Amigurumi
ANIMAL HATS
for 18-Inch Dolls

**20 Crocheted Animal Hat Patterns
Using Easy Single Crochet**

Linda Wright

In memory of Grandma S. who shared my love of crochet

Also by Linda Wright
Toilet Paper Origami
Amigurumi Toilet Paper Covers
Amigurumi Golf Club Covers
Amigurumi Christmas Ornaments
Amigurumi Holiday for 18-Inch Dolls
Honey Pie Amigurumi Dress Up Doll with Picnic Play Set
Honey Bunny Amigurumi Dress Up Doll with Garden Play Mat
Chef Charlotte Amigurumi Dress Up Doll with Tea Party Play Set

All rights reserved. No part of this book may be reproduced, stored in a retrieval system, or transmitted, in any form or by any means, electronic, mechanical, photocopying, recording, or otherwise, without prior written permission from the publisher. Permission is granted to photocopy patterns and templates for the personal use of the retail purchaser.

Lindaloo Enterprises is not affiliated with American Girl®

Copyright © 2015 Linda Wright
Edition 1.1

Lindaloo Enterprises
P.O. Box 90135
Santa Barbara, California 93190
United States
sales@lindaloo.com

ISBN: 978-0-9800923-8-7
Library of Congress Control Number: 2015905098

Contents

Introduction 5 General Directions 6

Cat 20
Ladybug 29
Owl 23
Lion 32
Sheep 26
Panda 35
Bear 44
Tiger 38
Cow 47
Dog 41

Introduction

When I was writing *Amigurumi Animal Hats*, a book of animal hat patterns for babies and children, it struck me that similar hats would be adorable for dolls. With basic crocheting skills, moms and grandmas could whip them up in a flash for the little ones in their lives. Beyond that, it was my deep desire that these hats would inspire young girls to learn to crochet their own doll clothes and, in the process, learn a wonderful life skill. *Amigurumi Animal Hats for 18-inch Dolls* is perfectly suited for the beginning crocheter. These patterns use the most elementary stitches and techniques while delivering an incredibly cute result in a short amount of time.

Amigurumi (ah•mee•goo•roo•mee) is a Japanese term for crocheted toys—be it animals, people or even inanimate objects. It is a colorful and cartoonish style of stitchery that is so much fun that once you start, it's hard to stop! Amigurumi is done by crocheting in a continuous spiral using one primary stitch—the single crochet—which makes it easy to master. It is also a tight stitch that works up into a nice, sturdy hat.

These hats were designed for my American Girl® dolls, but there are many other 18-inch dolls with a similar 12-inch head circumference. Measure your doll just above the ears. If slight adjustments are needed, going up or down a hook size or adjusting your tension (tightness) will make a hat larger or smaller.

Amigurumi Animal Hats for 18-Inch Dolls is all about funky fashion—and just plain fun! Here are some ways you can change the pattens to create different looks:

- Swap pom poms on the ties for tassels and vice versa.
- Make braided ties instead of twisted cord.
- Omit the twisted-cord ties for a different aviator style. You can even sew pom poms right to the tips of the ear flaps.
- Make any ear-flap hat as a beanie simply by omitting the ear flaps and ties.

For more delightful doll hats, check out my companion book, *Amigurumi Holiday Hats for 18-Inch Dolls*!

General Directions

If you're new to crocheting, or if you need to brush up, the following pages include instructional diagrams for the stitches used in this book.

If you like to learn by watching, YouTube.com is a treasure trove of excellent crocheting tutorials. To find what you need, just search on the stitch you want to learn and, for the best results, include "crochet" in your search. For example, magic ring crochet (also known as the magic circle or magic loop), single crochet, or loop stitch crochet. Several embroidery stitches are used for finishing touches on the hats and these can also be found demonstrated on YouTube, for example, the French knot.

For a hand-picked source of tutorials, I have assembled a collection of my favorites on Pinterest. You can view them at www.pinterest.com/LindalooEnt/ on boards named "Amigurumi Tutorials" and "Embroidery Tutorials". There you can watch demonstrations for the stitches and techniques needed to make amigurumi animal hats for your dolls.

Amigurumi is meant to be crocheted rather tightly. Be sure to check your gauge at the beginning of each pattern.

This book uses U.S. crochet terms. If an instruction says sc, that is a U.S. single crochet—or a U.K. double crochet. Please refer to the stitch diagrams on the following pages to be sure you are making the stitches as intended.

Supplies

Yarn

All of the yarn used to make these hats, except for the lion's mane, is soft worsted-weight yarn marked as number 4. Look on the label for the yarn weight symbol containing a "4" in the middle of a ball of yarn. Soft yarns frequently include "soft" in their name. I primarily use Caron "Simply Soft", Red Heart "Soft", Lion Brand "Vanna's Choice" and Lion Brand "Cotton-Ease". A yarn that is made of acrylic fibers, or acrylic blended with cotton or wool, is an ideal choice because the hat will be colorfast, washable and hold its shape well. The yarns that I used for these projects are listed in the Resources section at the back of the book.

Scissors

You will need a small pair of sharp scissors.

Crochet Hook

All of these patterns have been designed for a U.S. H/8 (5 mm) crochet hook. You may need to go up or down a hook size to obtain the gauge. My absolute favorite hook is the Clover Soft Touch Crochet Hook (pictured below, center). I love the ergonomic grip which keeps my hand from going numb when crocheting for long periods of time and the shape of the head which inserts easily into a stitch.

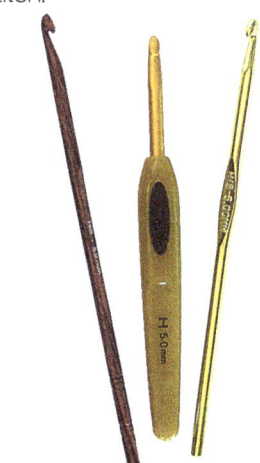

Yarn Needle

Yarn needles, or jumbo tapestry needles, have a large eye and a blunt point. They are made from metal or plastic. You will use one to sew the various pieces of your hat together and also to finish it off by weaving the loose ends into your work.

Stitch Markers

Stitch markers are used to keep track of where a round or row of crochet begins and ends. You can use a safety pin, bobby pin, paper clip or purchased stitch markers. I recommend the locking stitch markers that are shaped like safety pins. They are very easy, secure and convenient to use. Making the correct number of stitches is important, so count to double check if ever you're not sure.

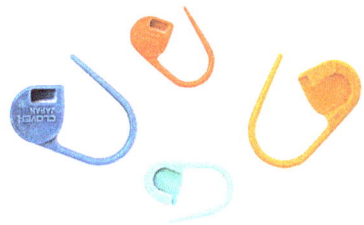

Buttons

Buttons are used for the animals' eyes. Sometimes a single set of buttons is used and sometimes buttons are stacked for a 2-tone effect. When buttons are stacked, use flat buttons with 2 or 4 holes in the surface. When unstacked, shank and half-round buttons are nice.

General Directions

Disappearing Ink Marking Pen

This terrific marking tool is a felt-tipped pen with ink (usually purple) that disappears in a day or so. Purchase it at a fabric store, craft store or online.

Row Counter

Well worth the investment, a row counter keeps track of what round of the pattern you are crocheting. A pencil and paper can also be used.

Straight Pins

Use standard dressmaker's pins or long corsage pins to hold pieces in place before sewing.

Sewing Needle & Thread

You will need these sewing box basics.

Styrofoam Ball

A 4-inch styrofoam ball makes a convenient hat form. Place hats on the ball to pin auxiliary features in place and mark their position.

Removable Notes

Use sticky notes to keep track of your place in a pattern. Every time you complete a round or a row, move the note down to reveal the next line of instructions. I wouldn't work without one!

Stuffing

There are very few stuffed pieces in these patterns. Polyester fiberfill is generally my favorite stuffing material, so if you have some on hand, you're all set. Otherwise, scraps of yarn will work just fine.

Ruler

For measuring and marking.

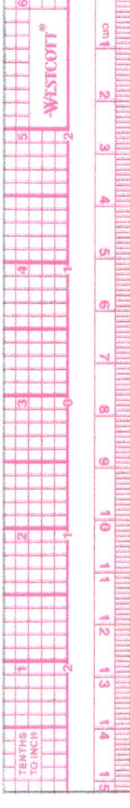

Crochet Stitches

SLIP KNOT

This is used to make a starting loop on the crochet hook.

1. Make a loop about 5 inches from end of yarn. Insert hook in loop and hook onto supply yarn (yarn coming from ball) at A.

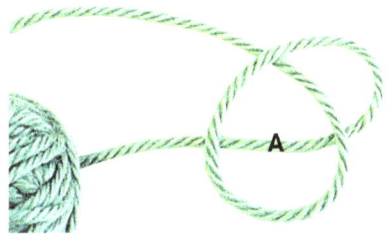

2. Pull yarn through loop.

3. Pull yarn ends to tighten loop around hook.

CHAIN (CH)

Start with a slip knot on hook.

1. Bring yarn **over** hook from back to front. Catch yarn with hook and pull it through the loop —

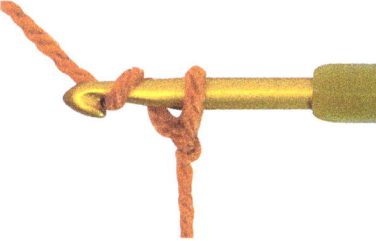

to look like this. One ch is done.

SINGLE CROCHET (SC)

This simple stitch is the primary stitch for amigurumi.

1. Insert hook in designated stitch. Note: Put hook under **both loops** that form v-shape at top of stitch unless otherwise instructed.

2. Yarn over and pull through the stitch (A).

You now have 2 loops on the hook.

3. Yarn over and pull through both loops on hook.

4. You now have 1 loop on hook and the sc stitch is done.

LOOP STITCH (LP ST)

The Loop Stitch is a variation of single crochet. The loops will form on the wrong side of the fabric (the side opposite the side you are facing). When the Loop Stitch is used for a hat, you will turn it wrong-side out when done. That way the loops will be on the outside — where you want them.

1. Insert hook in designated stitch, just as you do for a single crochet.

2. Wrap yarn around index finger of your yarn-holding hand to make a loop and lay loop on top of hook. Pull strands A and B through stitch C.

3. Yarn over and pull through all 3 loops on hook — A, B, and C.

4. The lp st is done.

SLIP STITCH (SL ST)

1. Insert hook in stitch. Yarn over and pull through stitch and through loop on hook (A and B).

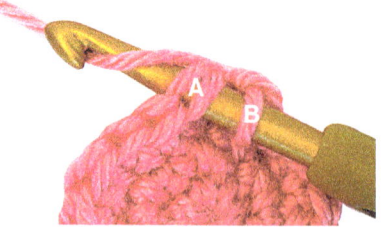

2. The sl st is done.

SINGLE CROCHET DECREASE (SC2TOG)

The instruction "sc2tog" means to use single crochet to join 2 stitches together. It is a way to decrease or make the item smaller.

1. Insert hook in stitch, yarn over and pull up a loop — to look like this.

2. Insert hook in next stitch, yarn over and pull up a loop — to look like this.

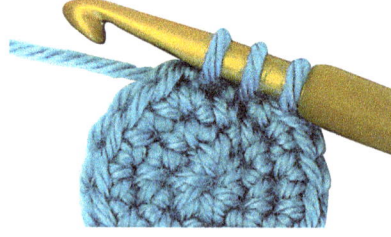

3. Yarn over and pull through all 3 loops on hook — to look like this. The sc2tog is done.

Techniques

★ MAGIC RING

Most all of my amigurumi begins with the magic ring. This is the way to get a nice, neat center when crocheting in the round. The magic ring is an adjustable loop that you can tighten — like magic! It's not difficult — and well worth it. (An alternative to the magic ring, if desired, is to chain 2. Then begin Round 1 by working into the 2nd chain from the hook instead of the ring.)

1. Make a ring a few inches from end of yarn. Grasp ring between thumb and index finger where the join makes an X. Insert hook in ring, hook onto supply yarn at Y and pull up a loop —

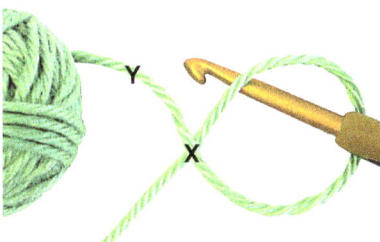

to look like this.

2. Chain 1 —

to look like this. This chain does not count as a stitch.

3. Insert hook into ring so you're crocheting over ring and yarn tail. Pull up a loop to begin your first single crochet —

and complete the single crochet.

4. Continue to crochet over ring and yarn tail for the specified number of single crochets for the 1st round.

5. Pull tail to close up ring. To begin the 2nd round, insert hook in 1st stitch of 1st round (see arrow).

BEGIN 2ND RND HERE

WORKING IN THE ROUND

Working in the round means crocheting in a continuous spiral. Most amigurumi is worked in this manner.

General Directions

USING STITCH MARKERS

It can be tricky to keep track of your place when working in the round, so be sure to use a stitch marker. The pattern will remind you! Place the stitch marker in the first stitch of a round — after completing the stitch. When you've crocheted all the way around, remove the stitch marker, make the next stitch, and replace the marker in the stitch just made. This will be the first stitch of the next round.

WORKING IN LOOPS

When a single crochet stitch is made, you will see 2 loops in a v-shape at the top of the stitch. To crochet the patterns in this book, insert your hook under **both loops**. Patterns that you encounter elsewhere may indicate to crochet in the front loops only or the back loops only for a different effect.

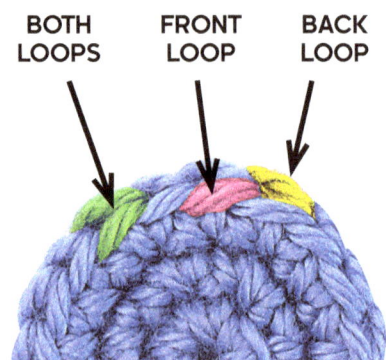

BOTH LOOPS   FRONT LOOP   BACK LOOP

MARKING THE EAR FLAPS

Counting clockwise from long tail of Hat, put stitch markers in stitches 10, 18, 37 and 45. Crochet Ear Flaps into the 7 stitches between each set of markers. (See purple stitches in photo below.)

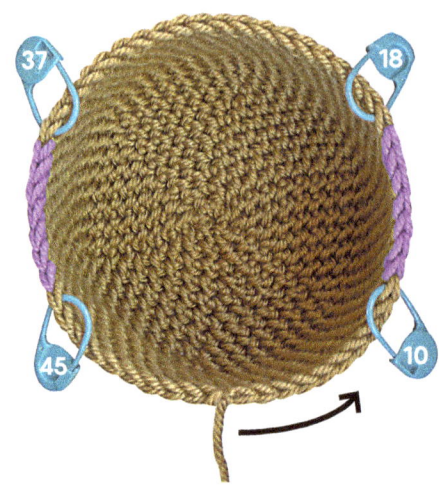

ATTACHING WITH SC

Attach yarn to hook with Slip Knot. Insert hook in indicated stitch. Complete sc as shown in Single Crochet tutorial, Page 9, Steps 2-4.

CHANGING COLORS

To change color while single crocheting, work last stitch of old color to last yarn over, yarn over with new color and pull through both loops on hook to complete the stitch.

FASTENING OFF

This is the way to finish a piece so that it won't unravel. When you're done crocheting, cut the yarn and leave a tail. Wrap the tail over your hook and pull it all the way through the last loop left on your hook. Pull the tail tight and it will make a knot.

SMOOTHING THE EDGE

When fastening off, the knot can make a small bump in the edge of your work so that, for example, a round shape will not look as round as it should. To make the edge smooth, thread the long tail in a yarn needle and insert the needle down through the center "V" of the next stitch. This little step makes a big difference!

General Directions   13

TWISTED CORD TIE

1. With crochet hook, pull 6 yarn strands through tip of Ear Flap —

and pull 1 side of loop all the way through until lower ends are even.

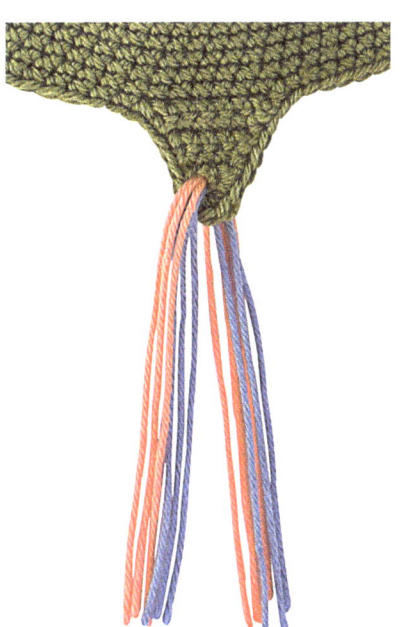

2. Place hat on a firm surface and weigh it down with a heavy book. Divide yarn into 2 groups of 6 strands. If 2 colors are used, make each group the same color.

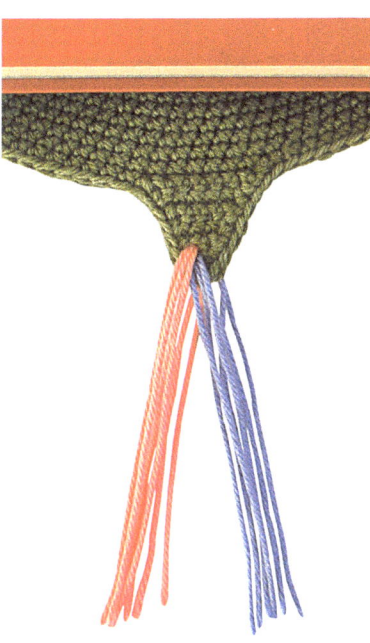

3. Hold a group in each hand grasping about 2 inches from Ear Flap — and twist yarn to the right.

4. When yarn has a good tight twist, wrap right group over left group —

and wrap **right over left** a few more times until all twisted yarn is wrapped.

5. Move your hands down 2 more inches, twist yarn and repeat Step 4. Continue twisting and wrapping until near end of strands. Tie all strands together with an overhand knot 6 inches from tip of Ear Flap. Trim ends even.

14 General Directions

SMALL POM POM

To embellish the ends of Twisted Cord Ties.

1. Copy and cut out 2 Small Pom Pom templates (see page 79). Glue templates to lightweight cardboard. (A cereal box is a good weight.) Cut along black lines. Hold cardboard templates together so that notches align. Wrap yarn evenly around ring, sliding yarn through notch and slit to begin each wrap.

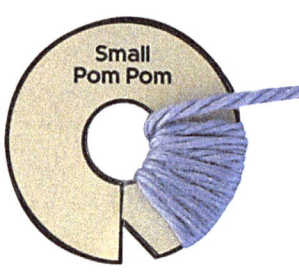

Wrap until inner circle is **almost filled** with yarn.

2. Insert Twisted Cord Tie into center of cardboard ring. Put 1 leg of scissors between cardboard rings and cut yarn apart around outer edge.

3. Slide a scrap of yarn between cardboard rings and tie the ends together very tightly.

4. Remove cardboard. Slide Pom Pom down cord to cover knot of Tie. Fluff yarn into a ball and trim surface into a nice, round shape.

MEDIUM & LARGE POM POM

To embellish the top of a Hat.

1. Copy and cut out 2 templates for desired Pom Pom size (see page 79). Glue templates to lightweight cardboard. (A cereal box is a good weight.) Cut along black lines. Hold cardboard templates together so that notches align.

2. Wrap yarn evenly around ring, sliding yarn through notch and slit to begin each wrap. Wrap until inner circle is **filled** with yarn.

3. Put 1 leg of a pair of scissors between cardboard rings and cut yarn apart around outer edge.

4. Slide a scrap of yarn between cardboard rings and tie the ends together very tightly. Leave long ends to use for tying Pom Pom to Hat.

5. Remove cardboard. Fluff yarn into a ball and trim surface into a nice, round shape.

FRINGE

1. Follow pattern instructions for length and quantity of yarn strands to be used. Put hook through desired stitch, catch strand(s) in the middle and pull part way through stitch to make a loop. (Photos below show fringe being made with 2 yarn strands.)

2. With hook in loop, lay yarn ends over hook.

3. Pull yarn ends all the way through loop. Take hold of ends and pull tight.

COUNTING ROUNDS

Periodically, it is good to count your rounds to ensure your place in a pattern. Fortunately, rounds are clearly defined and counting is easy. Each round makes a ridge. A groove separates the rounds. You need only to count the ridges. Take a look at the photo below to see that the circle has 5 rounds.

ASSEMBLING

The assembly stage of amigurumi hatmaking is an exciting time. This is when all pieces are sewn together and the project blossoms in cuteness! Thread a yarn needle with the long tail of your auxiliary piece (ear, snout, etc.) and use a whip stitch or running stitch to sew it to the hat. It's good to temporarily pin your pieces in place beforehand to decide where you like them the best.

WEAVING IN ENDS

The final assembly instruction for every pattern is to weave in the ends. This is the way to hide and secure all of your straggly yarn tails. Thread the yarn end into a yarn needle, then skim through the back of the stitches on the wrong side of your work. Continue for about 2 inches, then turn and double back to lock the yarn into place. Trim the end close. When you turn your work to the right side, you should not see the woven ends. They should be tucked into the middle of your crocheted fabric.

CLEANING

If you have used washable yarn, your hat will be easy to clean. Follow the laundry care instructions on the yarn label and wash as directed. Lay flat to dry.

Embroidery Stitches

STRAIGHT STITCH

A simple, single stitch. Come up from wrong side of fabric at A and go down at B.

RUNNING STITCH

The Running Stitch is formed by a detached series of Straight Stitches. Make it by running the needle up and down the fabric at a regular distance. Come up at A, down at B, up at C, down at D, up at E, down at F, etc.

FRENCH KNOT

Bring needle up from wrong side at A. Place needle close to fabric and wrap yarn around needle 3 times. Push needle down at a point near A.

LEOPARD'S SPOT

A variation of the Lazy Daisy or Detached Chain Stitch.

1. With a double strand of yarn, bring needle up from wrong side at A. Put needle back in at A and out at B, but don't pull the needle completely through. Wrap yarn around needle from left to right to form a loop.

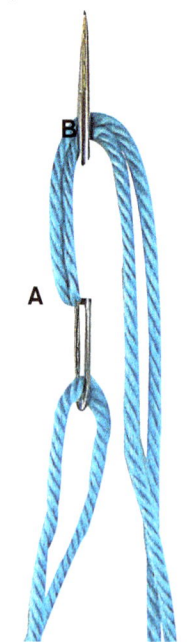

2. Pull needle out and loop will tighten. Don't pull too tight. Leave a bit of slack.

3. Put needle in at C, just over the loop.

4. Pull on sides of loop to spread it open —

and anchor it in place by stitching over loop at D and E.

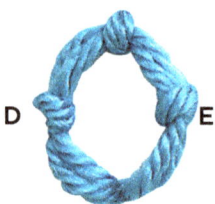

Note: To add interest, push loops into a variety of irregular circles before anchoring in place.

How to Measure your Gauge

Gauge is written as follows:

7 rnds of sc = 3" diameter circle

This means that when you've crocheted a 7-round flat circle of single crochet, the circle (or hexagon) you've created should have a 3" diameter. These hats all start with a flat circle, so when you have crocheted the first 7 rounds, measure your work. If the measurement is 3", your gauge is correct. To alter your gauge, adjust your crochet tension (tightness) or change to a larger or smaller crochet hook. It is very common for gauge to vary from person to person.

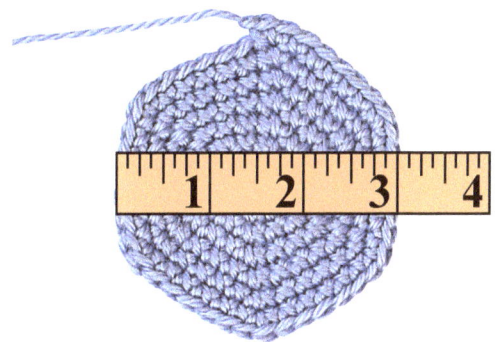

When laying flat, a completed hat should measure 4" from top to bottom (excluding ear flaps) and 6" across the center.

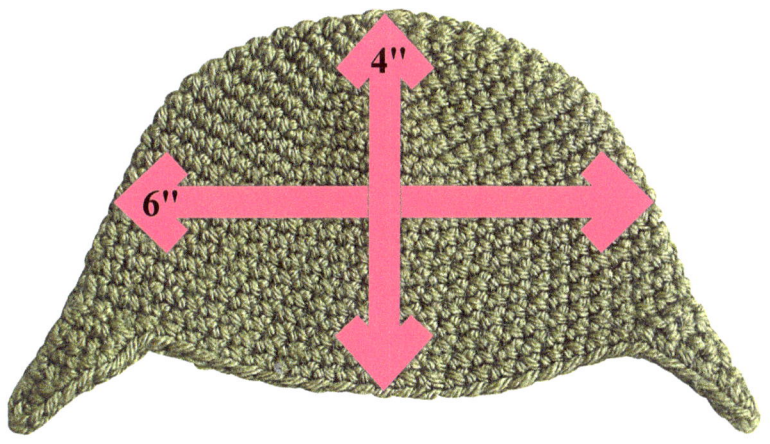

Abbreviations

Crochet patterns are written using abbreviations that save space and make the patterns easier to read.

The following abbreviations are used:

st	stitch
ch	chain
sc	single crochet
sl st	slip stitch
lp st	loop stitch
rnd	round
sc2tog	single crochet decrease
* *	repeat
( )	stitch count

How to Read a Pattern

Each round or row is written on a new line. Most rounds have a repeated section of instructions that are written between two asterisks *like this*. The instruction between the asterisks is to be repeated as many times as indicated before you move on to the next step. At the end of a round, the total number of stitches to be made in that round is indicated in parentheses (like this).

Let's look at a round from a hat:

Rnd 6: *sc in next 4 sts, 2 sc in next st* 6 times (36 sts).

This means:

Rnd 6	This is the 6th round of the pattern.
sc in next 4 sts	Make 1 single crochet stitch in each of the next 4 stitches
2 sc in next st	Make 2 single crochet stitches, both in the same stitch
6 times	Repeat everything between * and * 6 times.
(36 sts)	The round will have a total of 36 stitches.

So, following the instructions for Round 6, you will:

single crochet in the next 4 sts, 2 sc in the next st,
single crochet in the next 4 sts, 2 sc in the next st,
single crochet in the next 4 sts, 2 sc in the next st,
single crochet in the next 4 sts, 2 sc in the next st,
single crochet in the next 4 sts, 2 sc in the next st,
single crochet in the next 4 sts, 2 sc in the next st,

for a total of 36 stitches.

Cat

SUPPLIES

Worsted weight yarn in light gray (approx. 40 yards) and medium gray (approx. 40 yards) plus small amount of white, pink, and black

Size H/8 (5 mm) crochet hook or size needed to obtain gauge

2 black buttons, 5/8" diameter

Sewing needle and thread

Lightweight cardboard

Stitch marker

Yarn needle

GAUGE

7 rnds of sc = 3" diameter circle

HAT

The hat is worked by alternating 2 rnds of medium gray with 2 rnds of light gray. Change to alternate color in last st of every other rnd.

With medium gray yarn, make a magic ring, ch 1.

Rnd 1: 6 sc in ring, pull ring closed tight (6 sts).

Rnd 2: 2 sc in each st around. Place marker for beginning of rnd and move marker up as each rnd is completed (12 sts).

Rnd 3: *sc in next st, 2 sc in next st* 6 times (18 sts).

Rnd 4: *sc in next 2 sts, 2 sc in next st* 6 times (24 sts).

Rnd 5: *sc in next 3 sts, 2 sc in next st* 6 times (30 sts).

Rnd 6: *sc in next 4 sts, 2 sc in next st* 6 times (36 sts).

Rnd 7: *sc in next 5 sts, 2 sc in next st* 6 times (42 sts).

Rnd 8: *sc in next 6 sts, 2 sc in next st* 6 times (48 sts).

Rnd 9: *sc in next 7 sts, 2 sc in next st* 6 times (54 sts).

Rnds 10-20: sc in each st around. Fasten off.

EAR FLAP (MAKE 2)

Mark position of Ear Flaps (see page 12). Note: A chain 1 at the beginning of a row is for turning your work and does not count as a stitch.

Row 1: With light gray yarn, attach yarn in 1st st with sc, sc in next 6 sts. Place marker for beginning of row and move marker up as each row is completed (7 sts).

Row 2: ch 1, turn, skip next st, sc in next 6 sts (6 sts).

Row 3: ch 1, turn, skip next st, sc in next 5 sts (5 sts).

Row 4: ch 1, turn, skip next st, sc in next 4 sts (4 sts).

Row 5: ch 1, turn, skip next st, sc in next 3 sts (3 sts).

Row 6: ch 1, turn, skip next st, sc in next 2 sts (2 sts).

Row 7: ch 1, turn, skip next st, sc in next st (1 st).

Fasten off. Weave in end.

EDGE TRIM

Rnd 1: Using medium gray yarn, attach yarn at center back of Hat with sc. Sc in each st around perimeter of Hat making 3 sts at tip of each Ear Flap. Fasten off.

TWISTED CORD TIE (MAKE 2)

Cut three 24" strands of medium gray yarn and three 24" strands of light gray yarn. Follow instructions on page 13.

SMALL POM POM (MAKE 2)

With medium gray and light gray yarn, follow instructions on page 14.

Note: These are 2-tone Pom Poms. Hold both colors together when wrapping yarn around cardboard ring.

22 Cat

EAR (MAKE 2)

Make 1 ear piece with pink yarn and 1 ear piece with medium gray yarn.

With pink or gray yarn, chain 7 loosely.

Row 1: sc in 2nd chain from hook and each st across (6 sts).

Rows 2-3: ch 1, turn, sc in each st across (6 sts).

Row 4: ch 1, turn, sc2tog, sc in next 2 sts, sc2tog (4 sts).

Row 5: ch 1, turn, sc in each st across (4 sts).

Row 6: ch 1, turn, sc2tog twice (2 sts).

Row 7: ch 1, turn, sc in each st across (2 sts).

Row 8: ch 1, turn, sc2tog (1 st).

Fasten off. Weave in ends, weaving over any holes made by decreases.

Place pink and gray pieces wrong sides together. With gray yarn, sc pieces together around perimeter making 3 sts at each corner. Fasten off with long tail.

NOSE

With pink yarn, make a magic ring, ch 1.

Rnd 1: 4 sc in ring, pull ring closed tight (4 sts).

Sl st in next st. Fasten off with long tail.

SNOUT

With white yarn, make a magic ring, ch 1.

Rnd 1: 6 sc in ring, pull ring closed tight (6 sts).

Rnd 2: 2 sc in each st around. Place marker for beginning of rnd and move marker up as each rnd is completed (12 sts).

Rnd 3: *sc in next st, 2 sc in next st* 6 times (18 sts).

Rnd 4: *2 sc in next st, sc in next 2 sts* 6 times (24 sts).

Sl st in next st. Fasten off with long tail.

ASSEMBLY

Sew Ears slightly cupped to Hat. Sew Nose to Snout. With pink yarn, embroider straight stitch mouth (see diagram) on Snout. Sew Snout to Hat. With black yarn, embroider whiskers by making 1 long stitch for each whisker. Sew buttons to Hat for eyes. Weave in ends. ♦

Mouth

Owl

SUPPLIES

Worsted weight yarn in purple (approx. 45 yards) and pink (approx. 25 yards) plus small amount of white and yellow

Size H/8 (5 mm) crochet hook or size needed to obtain gauge

2 black buttons, 5/8" diameter

Sewing needle and thread

Stitch marker

Yarn needle

GAUGE

7 rnds of sc = 3" diameter circle

HAT

With purple yarn, make a magic ring, ch 1.

Rnd 1: 6 sc in ring, pull ring closed tight (6 sts).

Rnd 2: 2 sc in each st around. Place marker for beginning of rnd and move marker up as each rnd is completed (12 sts).

Rnd 3: *sc in next st, 2 sc in next st* 6 times (18 sts).

Rnd 4: *sc in next 2 sts, 2 sc in next st* 6 times (24 sts).

Rnd 5: *sc in next 3 sts, 2 sc in next st* 6 times (30 sts).

Rnd 6: *sc in next 4 sts, 2 sc in next st* 6 times (36 sts).

Rnd 7: *sc in next 5 sts, 2 sc in next st* 6 times (42 sts).

Rnd 8: *sc in next 6 sts, 2 sc in next st* 6 times (48 sts).

Rnd 9: *sc in next 7 sts, 2 sc in next st* 6 times (54 sts).

Rnds 10-14: sc in each st around; change to pink yarn in last st (54 sts).

Rnds 15-20: sc in each st around. Fasten off.

EAR FLAP (MAKE 2)

Mark position of Ear Flaps (see page 12). Note: A chain 1 at the beginning of a row is for turning your work and does not count as a stitch.

Row 1: With pink yarn, attach yarn in 1st st with sc, sc in next 6 sts. Place marker for beginning of row and move marker up as each row is completed (7 sts).

Row 2: ch 1, turn, skip next st, sc in next 6 sts (6 sts).

Row 3: ch 1, turn, skip next st, sc in next 5 sts (5 sts).

Row 4: ch 1, turn, skip next st, sc in next 4 sts (4 sts).

Row 5: ch 1, turn, skip next st, sc in next 3 sts (3 sts).

Row 6: ch 1, turn, skip next st, sc in next 2 sts (2 sts).

Row 7: ch 1, turn, skip next st, sc in next st (1 st).

Fasten off. Weave in end.

EDGE TRIM

Rnd 1: Using purple yarn, attach yarn at center back of Hat with sc. Sc in each st around perimeter of Hat making 3 sts at tip of each Ear Flap. Fasten off.

TWISTED CORD TIE (MAKE 2)

Cut three 24" strands of purple yarn and three 24" strands of pink yarn. Follow instructions on page 13.

OUTER EYE (MAKE 2)

With white yarn, make a magic ring, ch 1.

Rnd 1: 6 sc in ring, pull ring closed tight (6 sts).

Rnd 2: 2 sc in each st around. Place marker for beginning of rnd and move marker up as each rnd is completed (12 sts).

Rnd 3: *sc in next st, 2 sc in next st* 6 times (18 sts).

Rnd 4: *2 sc in next st, sc in next 2 sts* 6 times (24 sts).

Sl st in next st. Fasten off with long tail.

BEAK

With yellow yarn, ch 5.

Row 1: starting in 2nd ch from hook, sc2tog twice (2 sts).

Row 2: ch 1, turn, sc in each st across (2 sts).

Row 3: ch 1, turn, sc2tog (1 st).

Fasten off with long tail.

EAR (MAKE 2)

Cut two 6-inch strands of purple yarn and two 6-inch strands of pink yarn. Lay strands together and attach to one side of Hat using Fringe technique (see page 15). Trim to 1 inch. Repeat on other side of Hat.

ASSEMBLY

Sew buttons to Outer Eyes. Sew Eyes to Hat. Pinch corners of Beak into sharp points. Sew Beak to Hat. Weave in ends. ♦

Sheep

SUPPLIES

Worsted weight yarn in white (approx. 120 yards) and small amount of black

Size H/8 (5 mm) crochet hook or size needed to obtain gauge

2 brown buttons, 5/8" diameter

2 black buttons, 3/8" diameter

Sewing needle and thread

Lightweight cardboard

Stitch marker

Yarn needle

GAUGE

7 rnds of Hat = 3" diameter circle

HAT

The Hat is crocheted with alternating rounds of Single Crochet and Loop Stitch. Note: Loops will form on wrong side of work. Hat is turned loop-side out when done.

With white yarn, make a magic ring, ch 1.

Rnd 1: 6 sc in ring, pull ring closed tight (6 sts).

Rnd 2: 2 lp st in each st around. Place marker for beginning of rnd and move marker up as each rnd is completed (12 sts).

Rnd 3: *sc in next st, 2 sc in next st* 6 times (18 sts).

Rnd 4: *lp st in next 2 sts, 2 lp st in next st* 6 times (24 sts).

Rnd 5: *sc in next 3 sts, 2 sc in next st* 6 times (30 sts).

Rnd 6: *lp st in next 4 sts, 2 lp st in next st* 6 times (36 sts).

Rnd 7: *sc in next 5 sts, 2 sc in next st* 6 times (42 sts).

Rnd 8: *lp st in next 6 sts, 2 lp st in next st* 6 times (48 sts).

Rnd 9: *sc in next 7 sts, 2 sc in next st* 6 times (54 sts).

Rnd 10: *sc in next 20 sts, lp st in next 34 sts* (54 sts).

Rnd 11: sc in each st around.

Rnd 12: *sc in next 20 sts, lp st in next 34 sts* (54 sts).

Rnd 13: sc in each st around.

Rnd 14: *sc in next 20 sts, lp st in next 34 sts* (54 sts).

Rnd 15: sc in each st around.

Rnd 16: *sc in next 20 sts, lp st in next 34 sts* (54 sts).

Rnd 17: sc in each st around.

Rnd 18: *sc in next 20 sts, lp st in next 34 sts* (54 sts).

Rnd 19: sc in each st around.

Rnd 20: *sc in next 20 sts, lp st in next 34 sts* (54 sts). Fasten off.

EAR FLAPS (MAKE 2)

Mark position of Ear Flaps as follows: The section of hat that is plain sc (no loops) is the Sheep's face. The Ear Flaps are worked in the 1st 7 sts on each side of face. Note: A chain 1 at the beginning of a row is for turning your work and does not count as a stitch.

Row 1: With white yarn, attach yarn in 1st st with sc, sc in next 6 sts. Place marker for beginning of row and move marker up as each row is completed (7 sts).

Row 2: ch 1, turn, skip next st, lp st in next 6 sts (6 sts).

Row 3: ch 1, turn, skip next st, sc in next 5 sts (5 sts).

Row 4: ch 1, turn, skip next st, lp st in next 4 sts (4 sts).

Row 5: ch 1, turn, skip next st, sc in next 3 sts (3 sts).

Row 6: ch 1, turn, skip next st, lp st in next 2 sts (2 sts).

Row 7: ch 1, turn, skip next st, sc in next st (1 st).

Fasten off. Weave in end.

EDGE TRIM

Rnd 1: Using white yarn, attach yarn at center back of Hat with sc. Sc in each st around perimeter of Hat making 3 sts at tip of each Ear Flap. Fasten off.

Sheep

TWISTED CORD TIE (MAKE 2)

Cut six 24" strands of white yarn. Follow instructions on page 13.

SMALL POM POM (MAKE 2)

With white yarn, follow instructions on page 14.

SNOUT

With white yarn, make a magic ring, ch 1.

Rnd 1: 6 sc in ring, pull ring closed tight (6 sts).

Rnd 2: 2 sc in each st around. Place marker for beginning of rnd and move marker up as each rnd is completed (12 sts).

Rnd 3: *sc in next st, 2 sc in next st* 6 times (18 sts).

Rnd 4: *2 sc in next st, sc in next 2 sts* 6 times (24 sts).

Sl st in next st. Fasten off with long tail.

EAR (MAKE 2)

With white yarn, make a magic ring, ch 1.

Rnd 1: 6 sc in ring, pull ring closed tight (6 sts).

Rnd 2: *sc in next 2 sts, 2 sc in next st* 2 times. Place marker for beginning of rnd and move marker up as each rnd is completed (8 sts).

Rnd 3: *sc in next 3 sts, 2 sc in next st* 2 times (10 sts).

Rnd 4: *sc in next 4 sts, 2 sc in next st* 2 times (12 sts).

Rnd 5: *sc in next 5 sts, 2 sc in next st* 2 times (14 sts).

Rnd 6: *sc in next 6 sts, 2 sc in next st* 2 times (16 sts).

Rnd 7: sc in each st around.

Rnd 8: *sc in next 6 sts, sc2tog* 2 times (14 sts).

Rnd 9: *sc in next 5 sts, sc2tog* 2 times (12 sts).

Rnd 10: *sc in next 4 sts, sc2tog* 2 times (10 sts).

Rnd 11: *sc in next 3 sts, sc2tog* 2 times (8 sts).

Sl st in next st. Fasten off with long tail.

ASSEMBLY

Turn hat loop-side out. Flatten Ears and sew to Hat. Sew Snout to Hat. With black yarn, embroider a "Y" on Snout for nose. Stack black buttons on brown buttons and sew in place for eyes. Weave in ends. ♦

Nose

Ladybug

SUPPLIES

Worsted weight yarn in red (approx. 55 yards) and black (approx. 15 yards) plus small amount of white

Size H/8 (5 mm) crochet hook or size needed to obtain gauge

Disappearing ink marking pen

2 black buttons, 1/4" diameter

2 white buttons, 1/2" diameter

Sewing needle and thread

10mm flat black sequins

Black seed beads

Stitch marker

Yarn needle

GAUGE

7 rnds of sc = 3" diameter circle

HAT

With red yarn, make a magic ring, ch 1.

Rnd 1: 6 sc in ring, pull ring closed tight (6 sts).

Rnd 2: 2 sc in each st around. Place marker for beginning of rnd and move marker up as each rnd is completed (12 sts).

Rnd 3: *sc in next st, 2 sc in next st* 6 times (18 sts).

Rnd 4: *sc in next 2 sts, 2 sc in next st* 6 times (24 sts).

Rnd 5: *sc in next 3 sts, 2 sc in next st* 6 times (30 sts).

Rnd 6: *sc in next 4 sts, 2 sc in next st* 6 times (36 sts).

Rnd 7: *sc in next 5 sts, 2 sc in next st* 6 times (42 sts).

Rnd 8: *sc in next 6 sts, 2 sc in next st* 6 times (48 sts).

Rnd 9: *sc in next 7 sts, 2 sc in next st* 6 times (54 sts).

Rnds 10-20: sc in each st around.

Fasten off.

EAR FLAPS (MAKE 2)

Mark position of Ear Flaps (see page 12). Note: A chain 1 at the beginning of a row is for turning your work and does not count as a stitch.

Row 1: With red yarn, attach yarn in 1st st with sc, sc in next 6 sts. Place marker for beginning of row and move marker up as each row is completed (7 sts).

Row 2: ch 1, turn, skip next st, sc in next 6 sts (6 sts).

Row 3: ch 1, turn, skip next st, sc in next 5 sts (5 sts).

Row 4: ch 1, turn, skip next st, sc in next 4 sts (4 sts).

Row 5: ch 1, turn, skip next st, sc in next 3 sts (3 sts).

Row 6: ch 1, turn, skip next st, sc in next 2 sts (2 sts).

Row 7: ch 1, turn, skip next st, sc in next st (1 st).

Fasten off. Weave in end.

EDGE TRIM

Rnd 1: Using black yarn, attach yarn at center back of Hat with sc. Sc in each st around perimeter of Hat making 3 sts at tip of each Ear Flap. Fasten off.

TWISTED CORD TIE (MAKE 2)

Cut three 24" strands of red yarn and three 24" strands of black yarn. Follow instructions on page 13.

FACE

With black yarn, ch 2.

Row 1: 3 sc in 2nd ch from hook.

Row 2: ch 1, turn, 2 sc in next 3 sts (6 sts).

Row 3: ch 1, turn, *sc in next st, 2 sc in next st* 3 times (9 sts).

Row 4: ch 1, turn, *sc in next 2 sts, 2 sc in next st* 3 times (12 sts).

Row 5: ch 1, turn, *sc in next 3 sts, 2 sc in next st* 3 times (15 sts).

Row 6: ch 1, turn, *sc in next 4 sts, 2 sc in next st* 3 times (18 sts).

Continue across straight side making one sc in each st across. (Hold starting tail across straight side and crochet over tail as you work.) Sl st in next st. Fasten off with long tail.

ANTENNA (MAKE 2)

With black yarn, ch 8. Sc in 2nd ch from hook. Fasten off with long tail.

WINGS

Using disappearing ink marking pen, draw a line down center front and center back of hat.

With black yarn, sew along line with running stitch. Now sew in opposite direction to fill in the spaces, inserting needle through a bit of the stitches on either side to avoid gaps.

ASSEMBLY

Sew Face and Antennae to Hat. Stack black buttons on white buttons and sew in place for eyes. With white yarn, embroider a V-shaped mouth. Sew sequins randomly on Hat for spots as follows: bring sewing needle and thread up through Hat from wrong side, push needle through hole in sequin, insert seed bead on needle, then push needle back down through hole in sequin to wrong side of Hat. Weave in ends. ♦

Lion

SUPPLIES

Worsted weight yarn in golden-yellow (approx. 85 yards), and small amount of black plus super bulky Homespun yarn in variegated brown (approx. 20 yards)

Size H/8 (5 mm) crochet hook or size needed to obtain gauge

2 black buttons, 3/8" diameter

2 brown buttons, 5/8" diameter

Sewing needle & thread

Disappearing ink marking pen

Lightweight cardboard

Stitch marker

Yarn needle

GAUGE

7 rnds of sc = 3" diameter circle

HAT

With golden-yellow yarn, make a magic ring, ch 1.

Rnd 1: 6 sc in ring, pull ring closed tight (6 sts).

Rnd 2: 2 sc in each st around. Place marker for beginning of rnd and move marker up as each rnd is completed (12 sts).

Rnd 3: *sc in next st, 2 sc in next st* 6 times (18 sts).

Rnd 4: *sc in next 2 sts, 2 sc in next st* 6 times (24 sts).

Rnd 5: *sc in next 3 sts, 2 sc in next st* 6 times (30 sts).

Rnd 6: *sc in next 4 sts, 2 sc in next st* 6 times (36 sts).

Rnd 7: *sc in next 5 sts, 2 sc in next st* 6 times (42 sts).

Rnd 8: *sc in next 6 sts, 2 sc in next st* 6 times (48 sts).

Rnd 9: *sc in next 7 sts, 2 sc in next st* 6 times (54 sts).

Rnds 10-20: sc in each st around.

Fasten off.

EAR FLAP (MAKE 2)

Mark position of Ear Flaps (see page 12). Note: A chain 1 at the beginning of a row is for turning your work and does not count as a stitch.

Row 1: With golden-yellow yarn, attach yarn in 1st st with sc, sc in next 6 sts. Place marker for beginning of row and move marker up as each row is completed (7 sts).

Row 2: ch 1, turn, skip next st, sc in next 6 sts (6 sts).

Row 3: ch 1, turn, skip next st, sc in next 5 sts (5 sts).

Row 4: ch 1, turn, skip next st, sc in next 4 sts (4 sts).

Row 5: ch 1, turn, skip next st, sc in next 3 sts (3 sts).

Row 6: ch 1, turn, skip next st, sc in next 2 sts (2 sts).

Row 7: ch 1, turn, skip next st, sc in next st (1 st).

Fasten off. Weave in end.

EDGE TRIM

Rnd 1: Using golden-yellow yarn, attach yarn at center back of Hat with sc. Sc in each st around perimeter of Hat making 3 sts at tip of each Ear Flap. Fasten off.

TWISTED CORD TIE (MAKE 2)

Cut six 24" strands of golden-yellow yarn. Follow instructions on page 13.

SMALL POM POM (MAKE 2)

With variegated brown Homespun yarn, follow instructions on page 14.

EAR (MAKE 2)

With golden-yellow yarn, make a magic ring, ch 1.

Rnd 1: 6 sc in ring, pull ring closed tight (6 sts).

34 Lion

Rnd 2: 2 sc in each st around. Place marker for beginning of rnd and move marker up as each rnd is completed (12 sts).

Rnd 3: *sc in next st, 2 sc in next st* 6 times (18 sts).

Rnds 4-9: sc in each st around.

Fasten off with long tail.

MANE

You will need many 4-inch pieces of variegated brown Homespun yarn to make the Mane. To quickly cut the strands, wrap yarn widthwise around a 2" x 6" piece of cardboard. On one side, insert scissors between cardboard and yarn—and cut.

Flatten Hat and finger press so that center front meets center back. With disappearing ink marking pen, draw a line along crease from tip of one Ear Flap, over the top, to tip of other Ear Flap (see solid line, Figures A and B).

Work a row of fringe on each side of crease line (see dots, Figures A and B): Put hook through a st and follow instructions for Fringe (see page 15) using one 4-inch strand per st. (See Figure C.) Trim straggly ends.

SNOUT

With golden-yellow yarn, make a magic ring, ch 1.

Rnd 1: 6 sc in ring, pull ring closed tight (6 sts).

Rnd 2: 2 sc in each st around. Place marker for beginning of rnd and move marker up as each rnd is completed (12 sts).

Rnd 3: *sc in next st, 2 sc in next st* 6 times (18 sts).

Rnd 4: *2 sc in next st, sc in next 2 sts* 6 times (24 sts).

Sl st in next st. Fasten off with long tail.

NOSE

With black yarn, make a magic ring, ch 1.

Rnd 1: 5 sc in ring, pull ring closed tight (5 sts).

Sl st in next st. Fasten off with long tail.

ASSEMBLY

Sew Nose to Snout just below center and embroider straight stitch mouth (see diagram). Pull Snout gently at top and bottom to make a slight oval and sew to Hat. Stack black buttons on brown buttons and sew in place for eyes. Flatten Ears and sew to Hat between rows of Mane. Weave in ends. ♦

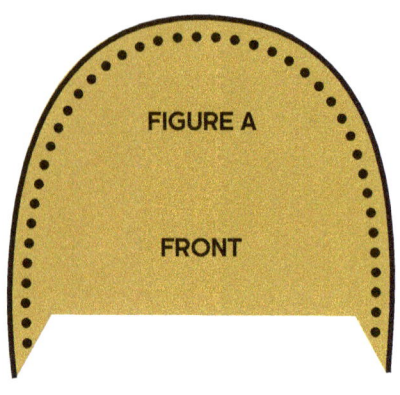

FIGURE A — FRONT

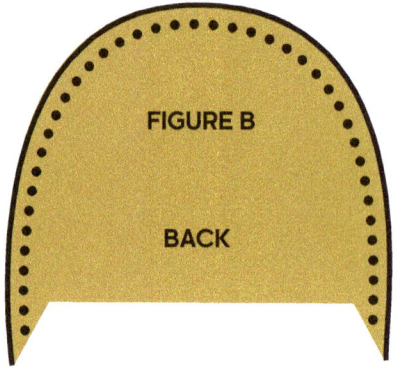

FIGURE B — BACK

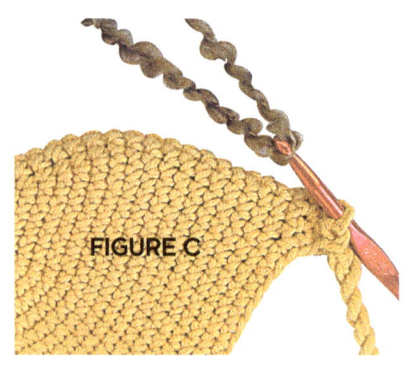

FIGURE C

Mouth

Panda

SUPPLIES

Worsted weight yarn in white (approx. 60 yards) and black (approx. 30 yards)

Size H/8 (5 mm) crochet hook or size needed to obtain gauge

2 white buttons, 3/4" diameter

2 black buttons, 1/2" diameter

Sewing needle & thread

Lightweight cardboard

Stitch marker

Yarn needle

GAUGE

7 rnds of sc = 3" diameter circle

HAT

With white yarn, make a magic ring, ch 1.

Rnd 1: 6 sc in ring, pull ring closed tight (6 sts).

Rnd 2: 2 sc in each st around. Place marker for beginning of rnd and move marker up as each rnd is completed (12 sts).

Rnd 3: *sc in next st, 2 sc in next st* 6 times (18 sts).

Rnd 4: *sc in next 2 sts, 2 sc in next st* 6 times (24 sts).

Rnd 5: *sc in next 3 sts, 2 sc in next st* 6 times (30 sts).

Rnd 6: *sc in next 4 sts, 2 sc in next st* 6 times (36 sts).

Rnd 7: *sc in next 5 sts, 2 sc in next st* 6 times (42 sts).

Rnd 8: *sc in next 6 sts, 2 sc in next st* 6 times (48 sts).

Rnd 9: *sc in next 7 sts, 2 sc in next st* 6 times (54 sts).

Rnds 10-20: sc in each st around.

Fasten off.

EAR FLAP (MAKE 2)

Mark position of Ear Flaps (see page 12). Note: A chain 1 at the beginning of a row is for turning your work and does not count as a stitch.

Row 1: With white yarn, attach yarn in 1st st with sc, sc in next 6 sts. Place marker for beginning of row and move marker up as each row is completed (7 sts).

Row 2: ch 1, turn, skip next st, sc in next 6 sts (6 sts).

Row 3: ch 1, turn, skip next st, sc in next 5 sts (5 sts).

Row 4: ch 1, turn, skip next st, sc in next 4 sts (4 sts).

Row 5: ch 1, turn, skip next st, sc in next 3 sts (3 sts).

Row 6: ch 1, turn, skip next st, sc in next 2 sts (2 sts).

Row 7: ch 1, turn, skip next st, sc in next st (1 st).

Fasten off. Weave in end.

EDGE TRIM

Rnd 1: Using black yarn, attach yarn at center back of Hat with sc. Sc in each st around perimeter of Hat making 3 sts at tip of each Ear Flap. Fasten off.

TWISTED CORD TIE (MAKE 2)

Cut three 24" strands of black yarn and three 24" strands of white yarn. Follow instructions on page 13.

MEDIUM POM POM (MAKE 2)

With black yarn, follow instructions on page 14.

EYE RIM (MAKE 2)

The Eye Rim is made in 2 parts.

Part A

With black yarn, make a magic ring, ch 1.

Rnd 1: 6 sc in ring, pull ring closed tight (6 sts).

Rnd 2: 2 sc in each st around. Place marker for beginning of rnd

Panda

and move marker up as each rnd is completed (12 sts).

Rnd 3: *2 sc in next st, sc in next st* 6 times (18 sts).

Sl st in next st. Fasten off with long tail.

Part B

With black yarn, ch 2.

Row 1: 3 sc in 2nd ch from hook (3 sts).

Row 2: ch 1, turn, 2 sc in each st across (6 sts).

Row 3: ch 1, turn, *2 sc in next st, sc in next st* 3 times (9 sts).

Fasten off with long tail. Place straight side of Part B anywhere against side of Part A and sew together.

SNOUT

With white yarn, make a magic ring, ch 1.

Rnd 1: 6 sc in ring, pull ring closed tight (6 sts).

Rnd 2: 2 sc in each st around. Place marker for beginning of rnd and move marker up as each rnd is completed (12 sts).

Rnd 3: *sc in next st, 2 sc in next st* 6 times (18 sts).

Sl st in next st. Fasten off with long tail.

NOSE

With black yarn, make a magic ring, ch 1.

Rnd 1: 5 sc in ring, pull ring closed tight (5 sts).

Sl st in next st. Fasten off with long tail.

ASSEMBLY

Sew Nose to Snout and use black yarn to make one vertical stitch at bottom of Nose (see photo). Sew Snout to Hat. Tie Pom Poms to Hat for ears. Stack black buttons on white buttons and sew to Eye Rims. Sew Eye Rims to Hat. Weave in ends. ♦

Tiger

SUPPLIES

Worsted weight yarn in orange (approx. 70 yards) and black (approx. 20 yards) plus small amount of white

Size H/8 (5 mm) crochet hook or size needed to obtain gauge

2 black buttons, 1/2" diameter

Sewing Needle & Thread

Stitch marker

Yarn needle

GAUGE

7 rnds of sc = 3" diameter circle

HAT

With orange yarn, make a magic ring, ch 1.

Rnd 1: 6 sc in ring, pull ring closed tight (6 sts).

Rnd 2: 2 sc in each st around; change to black yarn in last st. Place marker for beginning of rnd and move marker up as each rnd is completed (12 sts).

Rnd 3: *sc in next st, 2 sc in next st* 6 times; change to orange yarn in last st (18 sts).

Rnd 4: *sc in next 2 sts, 2 sc in next st* 6 times (24 sts).

Rnd 5: *sc in next 3 sts, 2 sc in next st* 6 times (30 sts).

Rnd 6: *sc in next 4 sts, 2 sc in next st* 6 times; change to black yarn in last st (36 sts).

Rnd 7: *sc in next 5 sts, 2 sc in next st* 6 times (42 sts).

Rnd 8: *sc in next 6 sts, 2 sc in next st* 6 times; change to orange yarn in last st (48 sts).

Rnd 9: *sc in next 7 sts, 2 sc in next st* 6 times (54 sts).

Rnd 10-11: sc in each st around; change to black yarn in last st.

Rnd 12: sc in each st around; change to orange yarn in last st.

Rnds 13-15: sc in each st around; change to black yarn in last st.

Rnds 16-17: sc in each st around; change to orange yarn in last st.

Rnds 18-20: sc in each st around.

Fasten off.

EAR FLAP (MAKE 2)

Mark position of Ear Flaps (see page 12). Note: A chain 1 at the beginning of a row is for turning your work and does not count as a stitch.

Row 1: With orange yarn, attach yarn in 1st st with sc, sc in next 6 sts. Place marker for beginning of row and move marker up as each row is completed (7 sts).

Row 2: ch 1, turn, skip next st, sc in next 6 sts (6 sts).

Row 3: ch 1, turn, skip next st, sc in next 5 sts (5 sts).

Row 4: ch 1, turn, skip next st, sc in next 4 sts (4 sts).

Row 5: ch 1, turn, skip next st, sc in next 3 sts (3 sts).

Row 6: ch 1, turn, skip next st, sc in next 2 sts (2 sts).

Row 7: ch 1, turn, skip next st, sc in next st (1 st).

Fasten off. Weave in end.

EDGE TRIM

Rnd 1: Using black yarn, attach yarn at center back of Hat with sc. Sc in each st around perimeter of Hat making 3 sts at tip of each Ear Flap. Fasten off.

TWISTED CORD TIE (MAKE 2)

Cut three 24" strands of orange yarn and three 24" strands of black yarn. Follow instructions on page 13.

OUTER EYE (MAKE 2)

With white yarn, make a magic ring, ch 1.

Rnd 1: 6 sc in ring, pull ring closed tight (6 sts).

Tiger

Rnd 2: 2 sc in each st around. Place marker for beginning of rnd and move marker up as each rnd is completed (12 sts).

Sl st in next st. Fasten off with long tail.

SNOUT

With white yarn, make a magic ring, ch 1.

Rnd 1: 6 sc in ring, pull ring closed tight (6 sts).

Rnd 2: 2 sc in each st around. Place marker for beginning of rnd and move marker up as each rnd is completed (12 sts).

Rnd 3: *sc in next st, 2 sc in next st* 6 times (18 sts).

Rnd 4: *2 sc in next st, sc in next 2 sts* 6 times (24 sts).

Sl st in next st. Fasten off with long tail.

NOSE

With black yarn, make a magic ring, ch 1.

Rnd 1: 5 sc in ring, pull ring closed tight (5 sts).

Sl st in next st. Fasten off with long tail.

EAR (MAKE 2)

With orange yarn, make a magic ring, ch 1.

Rnd 1: 6 sc in ring, pull ring closed tight (6 sts).

Rnd 2: 2 sc in each st around. Place marker for beginning of rnd and move marker up as each rnd is completed (12 sts).

Rnd 3: *sc in next st, 2 sc in next st* 6 times (18 sts).

Rnds 4-7: sc in each st around.

Fasten off with long tail.

ASSEMBLY

Flatten Ears and sew to Hat. Pull top and bottom of Snout to make an oval shape and sew to Hat. Sew Nose to Snout and embroider mouth with straight stitches. Sew Outer Eyes to Hat. Sew buttons to center of Outer Eyes. Weave in ends. ♦

Mouth

Dog

SUPPLIES

Worsted weight yarn in tan fleck (approx. 70 yards) plus small amount of brown fleck and black

Size H/8 (5 mm) crochet hook or size needed to obtain gauge

3 black buttons, 5/8" diameter (a half-ball button for nose is best)

Sewing needle and thread

Cardboard scrap

Stitch marker

Yarn needle

GAUGE

7 rnds of sc = 3" diameter circle

HAT

With tan fleck yarn, make a magic ring, ch 1.

Rnd 1: 6 sc in ring, pull ring closed tight (6 sts).

Rnd 2: 2 sc in each st around. Place marker for beginning of rnd and move marker up as each rnd is completed (12 sts).

Rnd 3: *sc in next st, 2 sc in next st* 6 times (18 sts).

Rnd 4: *sc in next 2 sts, 2 sc in next st* 6 times (24 sts).

Rnd 5: *sc in next 3 sts, 2 sc in next st* 6 times (30 sts).

Rnd 6: *sc in next 4 sts, 2 sc in next st* 6 times (36 sts).

Rnd 7: *sc in next 5 sts, 2 sc in next st* 6 times (42 sts).

Rnd 8: *sc in next 6 sts, 2 sc in next st* 6 times (48 sts).

Rnd 9: *sc in next 7 sts, 2 sc in next st* 6 times (54 sts).

Rnds 10-20: sc in each st around.

Fasten off.

EAR FLAP (MAKE 2)

Mark position of Ear Flaps (see page 12). Note: A chain 1 at the beginning of a row is for turning your work and does not count as a stitch.

Row 1: With tan fleck yarn, attach yarn in 1st st with sc, sc in next 6 sts. Place marker for beginning of row and move marker up as each row is completed (7 sts).

Row 2: ch 1, turn, skip next st, sc in next 6 sts (6 sts).

Row 3: ch 1, turn, skip next st, sc in next 5 sts (5 sts).

Row 4: ch 1, turn, skip next st, sc in next 4 sts (4 sts).

Row 5: ch 1, turn, skip next st, sc in next 3 sts (3 sts).

Row 6: ch 1, turn, skip next st, sc in next 2 sts (2 sts).

Row 7: ch 1, turn, skip next st, sc in next st (1 st).

Fasten off. Weave in end.

EDGE TRIM

Rnd 1: Using tan fleck yarn, attach yarn at center back of Hat with sc. Sc in each st around perimeter of Hat making 3 sts at tip of each Ear Flap. Fasten off.

TWISTED CORD TIE (MAKE 2)

Cut three 24" strands of tan fleck yarn and three 24" strands of brown fleck yarn. Follow instructions on page 13.

SMALL POM POM (MAKE 2)

With tan fleck yarn, follow instructions on page 14.

EAR (MAKE 2)

Cut a rectangle of cardboard measuring 4" x 12". Wrap brown fleck yarn lengthwise around cardboard 12 times. Carefully slide yarn off cardboard. Using a scrap of matching yarn, tie bundle together tightly around the middle. Cut loops open. (See Figure A.)

SNOUT

Cut a square of cardboard measuring 2 1/2" x 2 1/2". Wrap tan fleck yarn around cardboard 20 times. Carefully slide yarn off cardboard. Cut two 12" strands of black yarn. Use the double strand of black yarn to tie bundle together tightly around the middle. Wrap tails to opposite side and tie again. Cut loops open. (See Figure B.)

ASSEMBLY

Using black tails, tie Snout in place on Hat so that the black yarn tied around center is vertical. Tie Ears to Hat. Sew 2 buttons in place for eyes. Flatten yarn at top of Snout and sew button in place for nose. For eyebrows, embroider straight stitches over each eye (see Eyebrow Guide). Trim stray strands on Snout. Trim Ears even with tip of Ear Flaps. Weave in ends. ♦

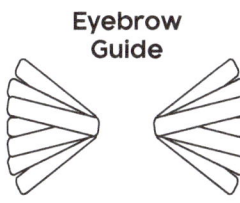
Eyebrow Guide

EAR

Figure A

SNOUT

Figure B

Dog 43

Bear

SUPPLIES

Worsted weight yarn in brown (approx. 60 yards) and tan (approx. 20 yards) plus small amount of black

Size H/8 (5 mm) crochet hook or size needed to obtain gauge

2 black buttons, 1/2" diameter

Sewing needle and thread

Lightweight cardboard

Stitch marker

Yarn needle

GAUGE

7 rnds of sc = 3" diameter circle

HAT

With brown yarn, make a magic ring, ch 1.

Rnd 1: 6 sc in ring, pull ring closed tight (6 sts).

Rnd 2: 2 sc in each st around. Place marker for beginning of rnd and move marker up as each rnd is completed (12 sts).

Rnd 3: *sc in next st, 2 sc in next st* 6 times (18 sts).

Rnd 4: *sc in next 2 sts, 2 sc in next st* 6 times (24 sts).

Rnd 5: *sc in next 3 sts, 2 sc in next st* 6 times (30 sts).

Rnd 6: *sc in next 4 sts, 2 sc in next st* 6 times (36 sts).

Rnd 7: *sc in next 5 sts, 2 sc in next st* 6 times (42 sts).

Rnd 8: *sc in next 6 sts, 2 sc in next st* 6 times (48 sts).

Rnd 9: *sc in next 7 sts, 2 sc in next st* 6 times (54 sts).

Rnds 10-20: sc in each st around.

Fasten off.

EAR FLAP (MAKE 2)

Mark position of Ear Flaps (see page 12). Note: A chain 1 at the beginning of a row is for turning your work and does not count as a stitch.

Row 1: With brown yarn, attach yarn in 1st st with sc, sc in next 6 sts. Place marker for beginning of row and move marker up as each row is completed (7 sts).

Row 2: ch 1, turn, skip next st, sc in next 6 sts (6 sts).

Row 3: ch 1, turn, skip next st, sc in next 5 sts (5 sts).

Row 4: ch 1, turn, skip next st, sc in next 4 sts (4 sts).

Row 5: ch 1, turn, skip next st, sc in next 3 sts (3 sts).

Row 6: ch 1, turn, skip next st, sc in next 2 sts (2 sts).

Row 7: ch 1, turn, skip next st, sc in next st (1 st).

Fasten off. Weave in end.

EDGE TRIM

Rnd 1: Using tan yarn, attach yarn at center back of Hat with sc. Sc in each st around perimeter of Hat making 3 sts at tip of each Ear Flap. Fasten off.

TWISTED CORD TIE (MAKE 2)

Cut three 24" strands of brown yarn and three 24" strands of tan yarn. Follow instructions on page 13.

SMALL POM POM (MAKE 2)

With brown and tan yarn, follow instructions on page 14.

Note: These are 2-tone Pom Poms. Hold both colors together when wrapping yarn around cardboard ring.

SNOUT

With tan yarn, make a magic ring, ch 1.

Rnd 1: 6 sc in ring, pull ring closed tight (6 sts).

46 Bear

Rnd 2: 2 sc in each st around. Place marker for beginning of rnd and move marker up as each rnd is completed (12 sts).

Rnd 3: *sc in next st, 2 sc in next st* 6 times (18 sts).

Rnd 4: *2 sc in next st, sc in next 2 sts* 6 times (24 sts).

Sl st in next st. Fasten off with long tail.

NOSE

With black yarn, make a magic ring, ch 1.

Rnd 1: 8 sc in ring, pull ring closed tight (8 sts).

Sl st in next st. Fasten off with long tail. Pinch circle at location of long tail to make a teardrop shape.

OUTER EYE (MAKE 2)

With tan yarn, make a magic ring, ch 1.

Rnd 1: 4 sc in ring, pull ring closed tight (4 sts).

Rnd 2: 2 sc in each st around (8 sts).

Sl st in next st. Fasten off with long tail.

EAR (MAKE 2)

Make 1 ear piece with tan yarn and 1 ear piece with brown yarn.

With tan or brown yarn, ch 2.

Row 1: 3 sc in 2nd ch from hook.

Row 2: ch 1, turn, 2 sc in next 3 sts (6 sts).

Row 3: ch 1, turn, *sc in next st, 2 sc in next st* 3 times (9 sts).

Row 4: ch 1, turn, *sc in next 2 sts, 2 sc in next st* 3 times (12 sts).

Fasten off. Weave in ends.

Place tan and brown pieces wrong sides together. With brown yarn, sc pieces together around perimeter making 3 sts at each corner. Fasten off with long tail.

ASSEMBLY

Sew Ears, Outer Eyes and Snout to Hat. Sew Nose to Snout and embroider mouth (see diagram below). Sew buttons to center of Outer Eyes. Weave in ends. ♦

Mouth

Cow

SUPPLIES

Worsted weight yarn in white (approx. 50 yards) and black (approx. 55 yards) plus small amount of pink and brown

Size H/8 (5 mm) crochet hook or size needed to obtain gauge

2 black buttons, 3/8" diameter

2 brown buttons, 5/8" diameter

Sewing needle and thread

Lightweight cardboard

Stitch marker

Yarn needle

GAUGE

7 rnds of sc = 3" diameter circle

HAT

With white yarn, make a magic ring, ch 1.

Rnd 1: 6 sc in ring, pull ring closed tight (6 sts).

Rnd 2: 2 sc in each st around. Place marker for beginning of rnd and move marker up as each rnd is completed (12 sts).

Rnd 3: *sc in next st, 2 sc in next st* 6 times (18 sts).

Rnd 4: *sc in next 2 sts, 2 sc in next st* 6 times (24 sts).

Rnd 5: *sc in next 3 sts, 2 sc in next st* 6 times (30 sts).

Rnd 6: *sc in next 4 sts, 2 sc in next st* 6 times (36 sts).

Rnd 7: *sc in next 5 sts, 2 sc in next st* 6 times (42 sts).

Rnd 8: *sc in next 6 sts, 2 sc in next st* 6 times (48 sts).

Rnd 9: *sc in next 7 sts, 2 sc in next st* 6 times (54 sts).

Rnds 10-20: sc in each st around.

Fasten off.

EAR FLAP (MAKE 2)

Mark position of Ear Flaps (see page 12). Note: A chain 1 at the beginning of a row is for turning your work and does not count as a stitch.

Row 1: With black yarn, attach yarn in 1st st with sc, sc in next 6 sts. Place marker for beginning of row and move marker up as each row is completed (7 sts).

Row 2: ch 1, turn, skip next st, sc in next 6 sts (6 sts).

Row 3: ch 1, turn, skip next st, sc in next 5 sts (5 sts).

Row 4: ch 1, turn, skip next st, sc in next 4 sts (4 sts).

Row 5: ch 1, turn, skip next st, sc in next 3 sts (3 sts).

Row 6: ch 1, turn, skip next st, sc in next 2 sts (2 sts).

Row 7: ch 1, turn, skip next st, sc in next st (1 st).

Fasten off. Weave in end.

EDGE TRIM

Rnd 1: Using black yarn, attach yarn at center back of Hat with sc. Sc in each st around perimeter of Hat making 3 sts at tip of each Ear Flap. Fasten off.

TWISTED CORD TIE (MAKE 2)

Cut three 24" strands of pink yarn and three 24" strands of black yarn. Follow instructions on page 13.

SMALL POM POM (MAKE 2)

With pink yarn, follow instructions on page 14.

SNOUT

The Snout is worked around a foundation chain.

With pink yarn, ch 7 loosely.

Rnd 1: starting in 2nd ch from hook *sc in next 5 sts, 3 sc in next st* 2 times. Place marker for beginning of rnd and move marker up as each rnd is completed (16 sts).

Rnd 2: *sc in next 5 sts, 2 sc in next 3 sts* 2 times (22 sts).

Sl st in next st. Fasten off with long tail.

EAR (MAKE 2)

With black yarn, make a magic ring, ch 1.

Rnd 1: 6 sc in ring, pull ring closed tight (6 sts).

Rnd 2: *sc in next 2 sts, 2 sc in next st* 2 times. Place marker for beginning of rnd and move marker up as each rnd is completed (8 sts).

Rnd 3: *sc in next 3 sts, 2 sc in next st* 2 times (10 sts).

Rnd 4: *sc in next 4 sts, 2 sc in next st* 2 times (12 sts).

Rnd 5: *sc in next 5 sts, 2 sc in next st* 2 times (14 sts).

Rnd 6: *sc in next 6 sts, 2 sc in next st* 2 times (16 sts).

Rnd 7: sc in each st around.

Rnd 8: *sc in next 6 sts, sc2tog* 2 times (14 sts).

Rnd 9: *sc in next 5 sts, sc2tog* 2 times (12 sts).

Rnd 10: *sc in next 4 sts, sc2tog* 2 times (10 sts).

Rnd 11: *sc in next 3 sts, sc2tog* 2 times (8 sts).

Sl st in next st. Fasten off with long tail.

SPOT (MAKE 3)

Each Spot is made in 2 parts.

Part A

With black yarn, make a magic ring, ch 1.

Rnd 1: 6 sc in ring, pull ring closed tight (6 sts).

Rnd 2: 2 sc in each st around. Place marker for beginning of rnd and move marker up as each rnd is completed (12 sts).

Rnd 3: *sc in next st, 2 sc in next st* 6 times (18 sts).

Rnd 4: *2 sc in next st, sc in next 2 sts* 6 times (24 sts).

Sl st in next st. Fasten off with long tail.

Part B

With black yarn, ch 2.

Row 1: 3 sc in 2nd ch from hook (3 sts).

Row 2: ch 1, turn, 2 sc in each st across (6 sts).

Row 3: ch 1, turn, *sc in next st, 2 sc in next st* 3 times (9 sts).

Fasten off with long tail. Place straight side of Part B anywhere against side of Part A and sew together.

HORN (MAKE 2)

With brown yarn, make a magic ring, ch 1.

Rnd 1: 4 sc in ring, pull ring closed tight (4 sts).

Rnd 2: sc in next 3 sts, 2 sc in next st. Place marker for beginning of rnd and move marker up as each rnd is completed (5 sts).

Rnd 3: sc in next 4 sts, 2 sc in next st (6 sts).

Rnd 4: sc in next 5 sts, 2 sc in next st (7 sts).

Rnd 5: sc in next 6 sts, 2 sc in next st (8 sts).

Sl st in next st. Fasten off with long tail.

ASSEMBLY

With a double strand of black yarn, embroider 2 French knots on Snout. Sew Snout to Hat. Sew Spots to Hat: 1 on each side and 1 on back. Flatten Ears, fold in half lengthwise and stitch at open end to hold crease. Sew Ears to Hat. Stuff Horns with scraps of brown yarn and sew to Hat. Stack black buttons on brown buttons and sew in place for eyes. Weave in ends. ♦

Bee

SUPPLIES

Worsted weight yarn in yellow (approx. 35 yards) and black (approx. 35 yards) plus small amount of white and orange

Size H/8 (5 mm) crochet hook or size needed to obtain gauge

2 black buttons, 1/2" diameter

Sewing needle and thread

Stitch marker

Yarn needle

GAUGE

7 rnds of sc = 3" diameter circle

HAT

With yellow yarn, make a magic ring, ch 1.

Rnd 1: 6 sc in ring, pull ring closed tight (6 sts).

Rnd 2: 2 sc in each st around. Place marker for beginning of rnd and move marker up as each rnd is completed (12 sts).

Rnd 3: *sc in next st, 2 sc in next st* 6 times (18 sts).

Rnd 4: *sc in next 2 sts, 2 sc in next st* 6 times (24 sts).

Rnd 5: *sc in next 3 sts, 2 sc in next st* 6 times (30 sts).

Rnd 6: *sc in next 4 sts, 2 sc in next st* 6 times (36 sts).

Rnd 7: *sc in next 5 sts, 2 sc in next st* 6 times (42 sts).

Rnd 8: *sc in next 6 sts, 2 sc in next st* 6 times; change to black yarn in last st (48 sts).

Rnd 9: *sc in next 7 sts, 2 sc in next st* 6 times (54 sts).

Rnd 10: sc in each st around; change to yellow yarn in last st.

Rnds 11-12: sc in each st around; change to black yarn in last st.

Rnds 13-14: sc in each st around; change to yellow yarn in last st.

Rnds 15-16: sc in each st around; change to black yarn in last st.

Rnds 17-18: sc in each st around; change to yellow yarn in last st.

Rnds 19-20: sc in each st around.

Fasten off.

EAR FLAP (MAKE 2)

Mark position of Ear Flaps (see page 12). Note: A chain 1 at the beginning of a row is for turning your work and does not count as a stitch.

Row 1: With yellow yarn, attach yarn in 1st st with sc, sc in next 6 sts. Place marker for beginning of row and move marker up as each row is completed (7 sts).

Row 2: ch 1, turn, skip next st, sc in next 6 sts (6 sts).

Row 3: ch 1, turn, skip next st, sc in next 5 sts (5 sts).

Row 4: ch 1, turn, skip next st, sc in next 4 sts (4 sts).

Row 5: ch 1, turn, skip next st, sc in next 3 sts (3 sts).

Row 6: ch 1, turn, skip next st, sc in next 2 sts (2 sts).

Row 7: ch 1, turn, skip next st, sc in next st (1 st).

Fasten off. Weave in end.

EDGE TRIM

Rnd 1: Using black yarn, attach yarn at center back of Hat with sc. Sc in each st around perimeter of Hat making 3 sts at tip of each Ear Flap. Fasten off.

TWISTED CORD TIE (MAKE 2)

Cut six 24" strands of black yarn. Follow instructions on page 13.

OUTER EYE (MAKE 2)

With white yarn, make a magic ring, ch 1.

Rnd 1: 6 sc in ring, pull ring closed tight (6 sts).

Rnd 2: 2 sc in each st around. Place marker for beginning of rnd and move marker up as each rnd is completed (12 sts).

52 Bee

Sl st in next st. Fasten off with long tail.

ANTENNA (MAKE 2)

With black yarn, ch 10 loosely.

Row 1: sc in 2nd ch from hook and in each remaining ch across (9 sts).

Fasten off with long tail.

MOUTH

With orange yarn, ch 5.

Row 1: starting in 2nd ch from hook, sc2tog twice (2 sts).

Row 2: ch 1, turn, sc in each st across (2 sts).

Row 3: ch 1, turn, sc2tog (1 st).

Fasten off with long tail.

ASSEMBLY

With crochet hook, pull long tails of antennae to inside of hat and tie in place. Thread yarn needle with long tails of antennae and push needle up through entire length of antennae so that long tails are concealed in the sts. Cut off excess yarn. (This will give the antennae more structure.) Sew Outer Eyes to Hat. Sew buttons to center of Outer Eyes. Pinch corners of Mouth into sharp points. Sew Mouth to Hat. Weave in ends. ♦

Sock Monkey

SUPPLIES

Worsted weight yarn in gray heather (approx. 40 yards) and dark red (approx. 25 yards) plus small amount of off-white

Size H/8 (5 mm) crochet hook or size needed to obtain gauge

2 black buttons, 1/2" diameter

Sewing needle and thread

Lightweight cardboard

Stitch marker

Yarn needle

GAUGE

7 rnds of sc = 3" diameter circle

HAT

With off-white yarn, make a magic ring, ch 1.

Rnd 1: 6 sc in ring, pull ring closed tight (6 sts).

Rnd 2: 2 sc in each st around. Place marker for beginning of rnd and move marker up as each rnd is completed (12 sts).

Rnd 3: *sc in next st, 2 sc in next st* 6 times (18 sts).

Rnd 4: *sc in next 2 sts, 2 sc in next st* 6 times (24 sts).

Rnd 5: *sc in next 3 sts, 2 sc in next st* 6 times (30 sts).

Rnd 6: *sc in next 4 sts, 2 sc in next st* 6 times (36 sts).

Rnd 7: *sc in next 5 sts, 2 sc in next st* 6 times (42 sts).

Rnd 8: *sc in next 6 sts, 2 sc in next st* 6 times; change to red yarn in last st. (48 sts).

Rnd 9: *sc in next 7 sts, 2 sc in next st* 6 times (54 sts).

Rnd 10: sc in each st around; change to gray yarn in last st (54 sts).

Rnds 11-20: sc in each st around. Fasten off.

EAR FLAP (MAKE 2)

Mark position of Ear Flaps (see page 12). Note: A chain 1 at the beginning of a row is for turning your work and does not count as a stitch.

Row 1: Using gray yarn, attach yarn in 1st st with sc, sc in next 6 sts. Place marker for beginning of row and move marker up as each row is completed (7 sts).

Row 2: ch 1, turn, skip next st, sc in next 6 sts (6 sts).

Row 3: ch 1, turn, skip next st, sc in next 5 sts (5 sts).

Row 4: ch 1, turn, skip next st, sc in next 4 sts (4 sts).

Row 5: ch 1, turn, skip next st, sc in next 3 sts (3 sts).

Row 6: ch 1, turn, skip next st, sc in next 2 sts (2 sts).

Row 7: ch 1, turn, skip next st, sc in next st (1 st).

Fasten off. Weave in end.

EDGE TRIM

Rnd 1: Using red yarn, attach yarn at center back of Hat with sc. Sc in each st around perimeter of Hat making 3 sts at tip of each Ear Flap. Fasten off.

SNOUT

The Snout is worked around a foundation chain.

With off-white yarn, ch 7 loosely.

Rnd 1: starting in 2nd ch from hook *sc in next 5 sts, 3 sc in next st* 2 times. Place marker for beginning of rnd and move marker up as each rnd is completed (16 sts).

Rnd 2: *sc in next 5 sts, 2 sc in next 3 sts* 2 times (22 sts).

Sl st in next st. Fasten off with long tail.

MOUTH

With red yarn, ch 8. Fasten off with long tail.

EAR (MAKE 2)

With gray yarn, make a magic ring, ch 1.

Rnd 1: 6 sc in ring, pull ring closed tight (6 sts).

Rnd 2: 2 sc in each st around. Place marker for beginning of rnd and move marker up as each rnd is completed (12 sts).

Rnd 3: sc in each st around.

Sl st in next st. Fasten off with long tail.

TWISTED CORD TIE (MAKE 2)

Cut three 24" strands of red yarn and three 24" strands of off-white yarn. Follow instructions on page 13.

SMALL POM POM (MAKE 2)

With red yarn, follow instructions on page 14.

LARGE POM POM

With red yarn, follow instructions on page 14.

ASSEMBLY

Sew Mouth in a curve to center of Snout. Sew Snout and Ears to Hat. Sew buttons in place for eyes. Tie Large Pom Pom on top of Hat. Weave in ends. ♦

Penguin

SUPPLIES

Worsted weight yarn in black (approx. 55 yards) and white (approx. 25 yards) plus small amount of orange

Size H/8 (5 mm) crochet hook or size needed to obtain gauge

2 black buttons, 1/2" diameter

Sewing needle and thread

Lightweight cardboard

Stitch marker

Yarn needle

GAUGE

7 rnds of sc = 3" diameter circle

HAT

With black yarn, make a magic ring, ch 1.

Rnd 1: 6 sc in ring, pull ring closed tight (6 sts).

Rnd 2: 2 sc in each st around. Place marker for beginning of rnd and move marker up as each rnd is completed (12 sts).

Rnd 3: *sc in next st, 2 sc in next st* 6 times (18 sts).

Rnd 4: *sc in next 2 sts, 2 sc in next st* 6 times (24 sts).

Rnd 5: *sc in next 3 sts, 2 sc in next st* 6 times (30 sts).

Rnd 6: *sc in next 4 sts, 2 sc in next st* 6 times (36 sts).

Rnd 7: *sc in next 5 sts, 2 sc in next st* 6 times (42 sts).

Rnd 8: *sc in next 6 sts, 2 sc in next st* 6 times (48 sts).

Rnd 9: *sc in next 7 sts, 2 sc in next st* 6 times (54 sts).

Rnds 10-20: sc in each st around.

Fasten off.

EAR FLAP (MAKE 2)

Mark position of Ear Flaps (see page 12). Note: A chain 1 at the beginning of a row is for turning your work and does not count as a stitch.

Row 1: With black yarn, attach yarn in 1st st with sc, sc in next 6 sts. Place marker for beginning of row and move marker up as each row is completed (7 sts).

Row 2: ch 1, turn, skip next st, sc in next 6 sts (6 sts).

Row 3: ch 1, turn, skip next st, sc in next 5 sts (5 sts).

Row 4: ch 1, turn, skip next st, sc in next 4 sts (4 sts).

Row 5: ch 1, turn, skip next st, sc in next 3 sts (3 sts).

Row 6: ch 1, turn, skip next st, sc in next 2 sts (2 sts).

Row 7: ch 1, turn, skip next st, sc in next st (1 st).

Fasten off. Weave in end.

EDGE TRIM

Rnd 1: Using white yarn, attach yarn at center back of Hat with sc. Sc in each st around perimeter of Hat making 3 sts at tip of each Ear Flap. Fasten off.

TWISTED CORD TIE (MAKE 2)

Cut six 24" strands of white yarn. Follow instructions on page 13.

SMALL POM POM (MAKE 2)

With orange yarn, follow instructions on page 14.

BEAK

With orange, yarn, ch 7.

Row 1: starting in 2nd ch from hook, sc2tog, sc in next 2 sts, sc2tog (4 sts).

Row 2: ch 1, turn, sc2tog twice (2 sts).

Row 3: ch 1, turn, sc2tog (1 st).

Fasten off with long tail.

58 Penguin

UPPER FACE (MAKE 2)

With white yarn, ch 2.

Row 1: 3 sc in 2nd ch from hook.

Row 2: ch 1, turn, 2 sc in next 3 sts (6 sts).

Row 3: ch 1, turn, *sc in next st, 2 sc in next st* 3 times (9 sts).

Row 4: ch 1, turn, *sc in next 2 sts, 2 sc in next st* 3 times (12 sts).

Fasten off with long tail. Weave in short tail from starting point.

LOWER FACE

With white yarn, ch 17 loosely.

Row 1: sc in 2nd ch from hook and in each remaining ch across (16 sts).

Rows 2-5: ch 1, turn, sc in each st across (16 sts).

Fasten off with long tail.

ASSEMBLY

Sew Upper Face pieces to Lower Face. Sew Upper Face pieces together at center (where they meet) with 2 whip sts. With white yarn, sc around outer edge of Face. Sew Face, Beak and button eyes to Hat. Weave in ends. ♦

Bunny

SUPPLIES

Worsted weight yarn in beige (approx. 115 yards) plus small amount of pink and white

Size H/8 (5 mm) crochet hook or size needed to obtain gauge

2 black buttons, 1/2" diameter

Sewing needle and thread

Lightweight cardboard

Stitch marker

Yarn needle

GAUGE

7 rnds of sc = 3" diameter circle

HAT

With beige yarn, make a magic ring, ch 1.

Rnd 1: 6 sc in ring, pull ring closed tight (6 sts).

Rnd 2: 2 sc in each st around. Place marker for beginning of rnd and move marker up as each rnd is completed (12 sts).

Rnd 3: *sc in next st, 2 sc in next st* 6 times (18 sts).

Rnd 4: *sc in next 2 sts, 2 sc in next st* 6 times (24 sts).

Rnd 5: *sc in next 3 sts, 2 sc in next st* 6 times (30 sts).

Rnd 6: *sc in next 4 sts, 2 sc in next st* 6 times (36 sts).

Rnd 7: *sc in next 5 sts, 2 sc in next st* 6 times (42 sts).

Rnd 8: *sc in next 6 sts, 2 sc in next st* 6 times (48 sts).

Rnd 9: *sc in next 7 sts, 2 sc in next st* 6 times (54 sts).

Rnds 10-20: sc in each st around.

Fasten off.

EAR FLAP (MAKE 2)

Mark position of Ear Flaps (see page 12). Note: A chain 1 at the beginning of a row is for turning your work and does not count as a stitch.

Row 1: With beige yarn, attach yarn in 1st st with sc, sc in next 6 sts. Place marker for beginning of row and move marker up as each row is completed (7 sts).

Row 2: ch 1, turn, skip next st, sc in next 6 sts (6 sts).

Row 3: ch 1, turn, skip next st, sc in next 5 sts (5 sts).

Row 4: ch 1, turn, skip next st, sc in next 4 sts (4 sts).

Row 5: ch 1, turn, skip next st, sc in next 3 sts (3 sts).

Row 6: ch 1, turn, skip next st, sc in next 2 sts (2 sts).

Row 7: ch 1, turn, skip next st, sc in next st (1 st).

Fasten off. Weave in end.

EDGE TRIM

Rnd 1: Using beige yarn, attach yarn at center back of Hat with sc. Sc in each st around perimeter of Hat making 3 sts at tip of each Ear Flap. Fasten off.

TWISTED CORD TIE (MAKE 2)

Cut three 24" strands of beige yarn and three 24" strands of pink yarn. Follow instructions on page 13.

EAR (MAKE 2)

With beige yarn, make a magic ring, ch 1.

Rnd 1: 6 sc in ring, pull ring closed tight (6 sts).

Rnd 2: *sc in next 2 sts, 2 sc in next st* 2 times. Place marker for beginning of rnd and move marker up as each rnd is completed (8 sts).

Rnd 3: *sc in next 3 sts, 2 sc in next st* 2 times (10 sts).

Rnd 4: *sc in next 4 sts, 2 sc in next st* 2 times (12 sts).

Rnd 5: *sc in next 5 sts, 2 sc in next st* 2 times (14 sts).

Rnd 6: *sc in next 6 sts, 2 sc in next st* 2 times (16 sts).

Rnd 7: *sc in next 7 sts, 2 sc in next st* 2 times (18 sts).

Rnd 8: *sc in next 8 sts, 2 sc in next st* 2 times (20 sts).

Rnd 9: *sc in next 9 sts, 2 sc in next st* 2 times (22 sts).

Rnd 10-14: sc in each st around.

Rnd 15: sc in next 20 sts, sc2tog (21 sts).

Rnd 16: sc in each st around.

Rnd 17: sc in next 19 sts, sc2tog (20 sts).

Rnd 18: sc in each st around.

Rnd 19: sc in next 18 sts, sc2tog (19 sts).

Rnd 20: sc in each st around.

Rnd 21: sc in next 17 sts, sc2tog (18 sts).

Rnd 22: sc in each st around.

Rnd 23: sc in next 16 sts, sc2tog (17 sts).

Rnd 24: sc in each st around.

Rnd 25: sc in next 15 sts, sc2tog (16 sts).

Rnd 26: sc in each st around.

Rnd 27: sc in next 14 sts, sc2tog (15 sts).

Rnd 28: sc in each st around.

Rnd 29: sc in next 13 sts, sc2tog (14 sts).

Rnd 30: sc in each st around.

Rnd 31: sc in next 12 sts, sc2tog (13 sts).

Rnd 32: sc in each st around.

Rnd 33: sc in next 11 sts, sc2tog (12 sts).

Sl st in next st. Fasten off with long tail.

TIE

With pink yarn, make an 18-inch chain. Fasten off. Weave in ends.

SMALL POM POM

Note: This Pom Pom is for the bunny's tail.

With white yarn, use Small Pom Pom template but follow instructions for Medium and Large Pom Poms on page 14.

ASSEMBLY

Flatten Ears and sew to Hat. Sew buttons in place for eyes. With a double strand of pink yarn, embroider a "T" for the nose. Fasten Tie in a bow around Ear. Tie Pom Pom to center back of Hat. Weave in ends. ♦

Frog

SUPPLIES

Worsted weight yarn in green (approx. 85 yards) and pink (approx. 10 yards) plus small amount of white and raspberry

Size H/8 (5 mm) crochet hook or size needed to obtain gauge

2 black buttons, 1/2" diameter

Sewing needle & thread

Stuffing

Stitch marker

Yarn needle

GAUGE

7 rnds of sc = 3" diameter circle

HAT

With green yarn, make a magic ring, ch 1.

Rnd 1: 6 sc in ring, pull ring closed tight (6 sts).

Rnd 2: 2 sc in each st around. Place marker for beginning of rnd and move marker up as each rnd is completed (12 sts).

Rnd 3: *sc in next st, 2 sc in next st* 6 times (18 sts).

Rnd 4: *sc in next 2 sts, 2 sc in next st* 6 times (24 sts).

Rnd 5: *sc in next 3 sts, 2 sc in next st* 6 times (30 sts).

Rnd 6: *sc in next 4 sts, 2 sc in next st* 6 times (36 sts).

Rnd 7: *sc in next 5 sts, 2 sc in next st* 6 times (42 sts).

Rnd 8: *sc in next 6 sts, 2 sc in next st* 6 times (48 sts).

Rnd 9: *sc in next 7 sts, 2 sc in next st* 6 times (54 sts).

Rnds 10-20: sc in each st around. Fasten off.

EAR FLAP (MAKE 2)

Mark position of Ear Flaps (see page 12). Note: A chain 1 at the beginning of a row is for turning your work and does not count as a stitch.

Row 1: With green yarn, attach yarn in 1st st with sc, sc in next 6 sts. Place marker for beginning of row and move marker up as each row is completed (7 sts).

Row 2: ch 1, turn, skip next st, sc in next 6 sts (6 sts).

Row 3: ch 1, turn, skip next st, sc in next 5 sts (5 sts).

Row 4: ch 1, turn, skip next st, sc in next 4 sts (4 sts).

Row 5: ch 1, turn, skip next st, sc in next 3 sts (3 sts).

Row 6: ch 1, turn, skip next st, sc in next 2 sts (2 sts).

Row 7: ch 1, turn, skip next st, sc in next st (1 st).

Fasten off. Weave in end.

EDGE TRIM

Rnd 1: Using pink yarn, attach yarn at center back of Hat with sc. Sc in each st around perimeter of Hat making 3 sts at tip of each Ear Flap. Fasten off.

TWISTED CORD TIE (MAKE 2)

Cut three 24" strands of green yarn and three 24" strands of pink yarn. Follow instructions on page 13.

EYE RIM (MAKE 2)

With white yarn, make a magic ring, ch 1.

Rnd 1: 4 sc in ring, pull ring closed tight (4 sts).

Rnd 2: 2 sc in each st around (8 sts).

Sl st in next st. Fasten off with long tail.

OUTER EYE (MAKE 2)

With green yarn, make a magic ring, ch 1.

Frog

Rnd 1: 6 sc in ring, pull ring closed tight (6 sts).

Rnd 2: 2 sc in each st around. Place marker for beginning of rnd and move marker up as each rnd is completed (12 sts).

Rnd 3: *sc in next st, 2 sc in next st* 6 times (18 sts).

Rnd 4: *sc in next 2 sts, 2 sc in next st* 6 times (24 sts).

Rnds 5-9: sc in each st around.

Fasten off with long tail.

BOW

With pink yarn, ch 6 loosely.

Row 1: sc in 2nd chain from hook and in each remaining ch across (5 sts).

Rows 2-3: ch 1, turn, sc in each st across (5 sts).

Rnd 4: sc in each st around next 3 sides. Join with sl st to next st. Fasten off.

Weave ends into wrong side. With a scrap of yarn, tie tightly across center of rectangle. Wrap 1 end around center several times to make a pretty pinched middle. Knot ends together leaving long tails.

ASSEMBLY

Sew buttons to Eye Rims. Sew Eye Rims to front of Outer Eyes. Tie Bow to top of one Eye. Stuff Eyes and sew to Hat. With raspberry yarn, embroider a V-shaped mouth by making 1 large running stitch for each side. Weave in ends. ♦

Chicken

SUPPLIES

Worsted weight yarn in white (approx. 60 yards) plus small amount of red and yellow

Size H/8 (5 mm) crochet hook or size needed to obtain gauge

2 black buttons, 3/8" diameter

2 amber buttons, 5/8" diameter

Sewing needle and thread

Lightweight cardboard

Stitch marker

Yarn needle

GAUGE

7 rnds of sc = 3" diameter circle

HAT

With white yarn, make a magic ring, ch 1.

Rnd 1: 6 sc in ring, pull ring closed tight (6 sts).

Rnd 2: 2 sc in each st around. Place marker for beginning of rnd and move marker up as each rnd is completed (12 sts).

Rnd 3: *sc in next st, 2 sc in next st* 6 times (18 sts).

Rnd 4: *sc in next 2 sts, 2 sc in next st* 6 times (24 sts).

Rnd 5: *sc in next 3 sts, 2 sc in next st* 6 times (30 sts).

Rnd 6: *sc in next 4 sts, 2 sc in next st* 6 times (36 sts).

Rnd 7: *sc in next 5 sts, 2 sc in next st* 6 times (42 sts).

Rnd 8: *sc in next 6 sts, 2 sc in next st* 6 times (48 sts).

Rnd 9: *sc in next 7 sts, 2 sc in next st* 6 times (54 sts).

Rnds 10-20: sc in each st around.

Fasten off.

EAR FLAP (MAKE 2)

Mark position of Ear Flaps (see page 12). Note: A chain 1 at the beginning of a row is for turning your work and does not count as a stitch.

Row 1: With white yarn, attach yarn in 1st st with sc, sc in next 6 sts. Place marker for beginning of row and move marker up as each row is completed (7 sts).

Row 2: ch 1, turn, skip next st, sc in next 6 sts (6 sts).

Row 3: ch 1, turn, skip next st, sc in next 5 sts (5 sts).

Row 4: ch 1, turn, skip next st, sc in next 4 sts (4 sts).

Row 5: ch 1, turn, skip next st, sc in next 3 sts (3 sts).

Row 6: ch 1, turn, skip next st, sc in next 2 sts (2 sts).

Row 7: ch 1, turn, skip next st, sc in next st (1 st).

Fasten off. Weave in end.

EDGE TRIM

Rnd 1: Using white yarn, attach yarn at center back of Hat with sc. Sc in each st around perimeter of Hat making 3 sts at tip of each Ear Flap. Fasten off.

TWISTED CORD TIE (MAKE 2)

Cut six 24" strands of yellow yarn. Follow instructions on page 13.

MEDIUM POM POM

With red yarn, follow instructions on page 14.

BEAK (MAKE 2)

With yellow yarn, make a magic ring, ch 1.

Rnd 1: 4 sc in ring, pull ring closed tight (4 sts).

Rnd 2: sc in next 3 sts, 2 sc in next st. Place marker for beginning of rnd and move marker up as each rnd is completed (5 sts).

Rnd 3: sc in next 4 sts, 2 sc in next st (6 sts).

Rnd 4: sc in next 5 sts, 2 sc in next st (7 sts).

Rnd 5: sc in next 6 sts, 2 sc in next st (8 sts).

Rnd 6: sc in next 7 sts, 2 sc in next st (9 sts).

Sl st in next st. Fasten off with long tail.

ASSEMBLY

Flatten and stack Beak pieces. Sew the two adjoining edges together to make a hinge. Sew Beak to Hat. Stack black buttons on amber buttons and sew to Hat for eyes. Tie Pom Pom to top of Hat. Weave in ends. ♦

Octopus

SUPPLIES

Worsted weight yarn in aqua (approx. 110 yards) plus small amount of white

Size H/8 (5 mm) crochet hook or size needed to obtain gauge

2 black buttons, 1/2" diameter

Sewing needle and thread

Stitch marker

Yarn needle

GAUGE

7 rnds of sc = 3" diameter circle

HAT

With aqua yarn, make a magic ring, ch 1.

Rnd 1: 6 sc in ring, pull ring closed tight (6 sts).

Rnd 2: 2 sc in each st around. Place marker for beginning of rnd and move marker up as each rnd is completed (12 sts).

Rnd 3: *sc in next st, 2 sc in next st* 6 times (18 sts).

Rnd 4: *sc in next 2 sts, 2 sc in next st* 6 times (24 sts).

Rnd 5: *sc in next 3 sts, 2 sc in next st* 6 times (30 sts).

Rnd 6: *sc in next 4 sts, 2 sc in next st* 6 times (36 sts).

Rnd 7: *sc in next 5 sts, 2 sc in next st* 6 times (42 sts).

Rnd 8: *sc in next 6 sts, 2 sc in next st* 6 times (48 sts).

Rnd 9: *sc in next 7 sts, 2 sc in next st* 6 times (54 sts).

Rnds 10-21: sc in each st around.

Fasten off.

ARM (MAKE 8)

With aqua yarn, ch 31 loosely.

Row 1: sc in 2nd ch from hook and in each remaining ch across (30 sts).

Rows 2-3: ch 1, turn, sc in each st across (30 sts).

One arm is done. Without cutting the yarn, ch 31 and repeat Rows 1-3 to make 7 more Arms. You will end up with 8 curly Arms all in a row. Fasten off with long tail.

OUTER EYE (MAKE 2)

With white yarn, make a magic ring, ch 1.

Rnd 1: 6 sc in ring, pull ring closed tight (6 sts).

Rnd 2: 2 sc in each st around. Place marker for beginning of rnd and move marker up as each rnd is completed (12 sts).

Sl st in next st. Fasten off with long tail.

ASSEMBLY

Pin row of legs to hat, right sides together, matching center of leg strip to center back of hat. Sew in place. Sew buttons to center of Outer Eyes. Sew Eyes to Hat. Weave in ends. ♦

Snow Leopard

SUPPLIES

Worsted weight yarn in pale gray (approx. 65 yards) and black (approx. 25 yards) plus small amount of peach and white

Size H/8 (5 mm) crochet hook or size needed to obtain gauge

2 black buttons, 3/8" diameter

2 green buttons, 5/8" diameter

Sewing needle and thread

Lightweight cardboard

Stitch marker

Yarn needle

GAUGE

7 rnds of sc = 3" diameter circle

HAT

With pale gray yarn, make a magic ring, ch 1.

Rnd 1: 6 sc in ring, pull ring closed tight (6 sts).

Rnd 2: 2 sc in each st around. Place marker for beginning of rnd and move marker up as each rnd is completed (12 sts).

Rnd 3: *sc in next st, 2 sc in next st* 6 times (18 sts).

Rnd 4: *sc in next 2 sts, 2 sc in next st* 6 times (24 sts).

Rnd 5: *sc in next 3 sts, 2 sc in next st* 6 times (30 sts).

Rnd 6: *sc in next 4 sts, 2 sc in next st* 6 times (36 sts).

Rnd 7: *sc in next 5 sts, 2 sc in next st* 6 times (42 sts).

Rnd 8: *sc in next 6 sts, 2 sc in next st* 6 times (48 sts).

Rnd 9: *sc in next 7 sts, 2 sc in next st* 6 times (54 sts).

Rnds 10-20: sc in each st around.

Fasten off.

EAR FLAP (MAKE 2)

Mark position of Ear Flaps (see page 12). Note: A chain 1 at the beginning of a row is for turning your work and does not count as a stitch.

Row 1: With pale gray yarn, attach yarn in 1st st with sc, sc in next 6 sts. Place marker for beginning of row and move marker up as each row is completed (7 sts).

Row 2: ch 1, turn, skip next st, sc in next 6 sts (6 sts).

Row 3: ch 1, turn, skip next st, sc in next 5 sts (5 sts).

Row 4: ch 1, turn, skip next st, sc in next 4 sts (4 sts).

Row 5: ch 1, turn, skip next st, sc in next 3 sts (3 sts).

Row 6: ch 1, turn, skip next st, sc in next 2 sts (2 sts).

Row 7: ch 1, turn, skip next st, sc in next st (1 st).

Fasten off. Weave in end.

EDGE TRIM

Rnd 1: Using pale gray yarn, attach yarn at center back of Hat with sc. Sc in each st around perimeter of Hat making 3 sts at tip of each Ear Flap. Fasten off.

TWISTED CORD TIE (MAKE 2)

Cut six 24" strands of pale gray yarn. Follow instructions on page 13.

SMALL POM POM (MAKE 2)

With pale gray and black yarn, follow instructions on page 14.

Note: These are 2-tone Pom Poms. Hold both colors together when wrapping yarn around cardboard ring.

OUTER EYE (MAKE 2)

With black yarn, make a magic ring, ch 1.

Rnd 1: 6 sc in ring, pull ring closed tight (6 sts).

Snow Leopard

Rnd 2a: 2 sc in next 2 sts (4 sts).

Point: ch 2 and sc in 2nd ch from hook, sc in next st.

Rnd 2b: 2 sc in next 2 sts (4 sts).

Point: ch 2 and sc in 2nd ch from hook, sc in next st.

Sl st in next st. Fasten off with long tail.

EAR (MAKE 2)

With pale gray yarn, make a magic ring, ch 1.

Rnd 1: 6 sc in ring, pull ring closed tight (6 sts).

Rnd 2: 2 sc in each st around. Place marker for beginning of rnd and move marker up as each rnd is completed (12 sts).

Rnd 3: *sc in next st, 2 sc in next st* 6 times (18 sts).

Rnds 4-7: sc in each st around.

Fasten off with long tail.

SNOUT

With pale gray yarn, ch 5 loosely.

Row 1: sc in 2nd ch from hook and in each remaining ch across (4 sts).

Rows 2-8: ch 1, turn, sc in each st across (4 sts).

Row 9: ch 1, turn, sc2tog twice (2 sts).

Row 10: ch 1, turn, sc2tog (1 st).

Fasten off with long tail.

NOSE

With peach yarn, ch 5.

Row 1: starting in 2nd ch from hook, sc2tog twice (2 sts).

Row 2: ch 1, turn, sc2tog (1 st).

Fasten off with long tail.

ASSEMBLY

Flatten Ears and sew to Hat. Sew Snout to Hat. Sew Nose to Snout. Sew Outer Eyes to Hat. Stack black buttons on green buttons and sew to center of Outer Eyes. Using a double strand of black yarn, embroider mouth (see diagram). Using a single strand of white yarn, embroider whiskers.

For spots, use a double strand of black yarn and embroider Leopard's Spot stitches (see page 16) randomly around top, sides and back of Hat. Weave in ends. ♦

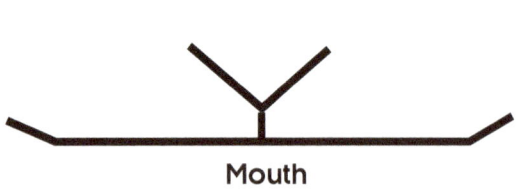

Mouth

Dinosaur

SUPPLIES

Worsted weight yarn in green (approx. 55 yards) and turquoise (approx. 30 yards) plus small amount of yellow and black

Size H/8 (5 mm) crochet hook or size needed to obtain gauge

Disappearing ink marking pen

2 black buttons, 3/8" diameter

2 yellow buttons, 5/8" diameter

Sewing needle & Thread

Stitch marker

Yarn needle

GAUGE

7 rnds of sc = 3" diameter circle

HAT

With green yarn, make a magic ring, ch 1.

Rnd 1: 6 sc in ring, pull ring closed tight (6 sts).

Rnd 2: 2 sc in each st around. Place marker for beginning of rnd and move marker up as each rnd is completed (12 sts).

Rnd 3: *sc in next st, 2 sc in next st* 6 times (18 sts).

Rnd 4: *sc in next 2 sts, 2 sc in next st* 6 times (24 sts).

Rnd 5: *sc in next 3 sts, 2 sc in next st* 6 times (30 sts).

Rnd 6: *sc in next 4 sts, 2 sc in next st* 6 times (36 sts).

Rnd 7: *sc in next 5 sts, 2 sc in next st* 6 times (42 sts).

Rnd 8: *sc in next 6 sts, 2 sc in next st* 6 times (48 sts).

Rnd 9: *sc in next 7 sts, 2 sc in next st* 6 times (54 sts).

Rnds 10-20: sc in each st around.

Fasten off.

EAR FLAP (MAKE 2)

Mark position of Ear Flaps (see page 12). Note: A chain 1 at the beginning of a row is for turning your work and does not count as a stitch.

Row 1: With green yarn, attach yarn in 1st st with sc, sc in next 6 sts. Place marker for beginning of row and move marker up as each row is completed (7 sts).

Row 2: ch 1, turn, skip next st, sc in next 6 sts (6 sts).

Row 3: ch 1, turn, skip next st, sc in next 5 sts (5 sts).

Row 4: ch 1, turn, skip next st, sc in next 4 sts (4 sts).

Row 5: ch 1, turn, skip next st, sc in next 3 sts (3 sts).

Row 6: ch 1, turn, skip next st, sc in next 2 sts (2 sts).

Row 7: ch 1, turn, skip next st, sc in next st (1 st).

Fasten off. Weave in end.

EDGE TRIM

Rnd 1: Using turquoise yarn, attach yarn at center back of Hat with sc. Sc in each st around perimeter of Hat making 3 sts at tip of each Ear Flap. Fasten off.

TWISTED CORD TIE (MAKE 2)

Cut three 24" strands of turquoise yarn and three 24" strands of yellow yarn. Follow instructions on page 13.

PLATE (MAKE 3)

With turquoise yarn, make a magic ring, ch 1.

Rnd 1: 6 sc in ring, pull ring closed tight (6 sts).

Rnd 2: *sc in next 2 sts, 2 sc in next st* 2 times. Place marker for beginning of rnd and move marker up as each rnd is completed (8 sts).

Rnd 3: *sc in next 3 sts, 2 sc in next st* 2 times (10 sts).

Rnd 4: *sc in next 4 sts, 2 sc in next st* 2 times (12 sts).

Rnd 5: *sc in next 5 sts, 2 sc in next st* 2 times (14 sts).

Rnd 6: *sc in next 6 sts, 2 sc in next st* 2 times (16 sts).

Rnd 7: *sc in next 7 sts, 2 sc in next st* 2 times (18 sts).

Sl st in next st. Fasten off with long tail. Flatten and pinch tip into nice point.

ASSEMBLY

Lay Hat flat and draw a line with disappearing ink marking pen along the center (see Figure A). Flip Hat over and repeat on other side. Stack black buttons on yellow buttons and sew in place for eyes. With black yarn, make 2 French Knots for nostrils. Sew Plates to Hat on center line. Note: I find it easiest to lay Plates on their side and whip stitch securely to Hat, then raise them up into position. Weave in ends. ♦

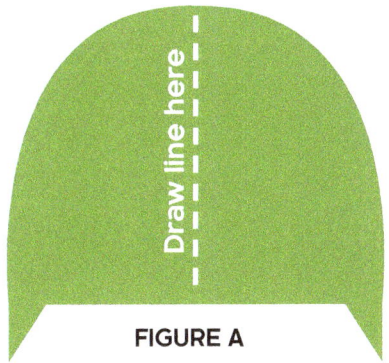

FIGURE A

Pig

SUPPLIES

Worsted weight yarn in pink (approx. 100 yards)

Size H/8 (5 mm) crochet hook or size needed to obtain gauge

2 black buttons, 1/4" diameter

2 black buttons, 1/2" diameter

Sewing needle and thread

Lightweight cardboard

Stitch marker

Yarn needle

GAUGE

7 rnds of sc = 3" diameter circle

HAT

With pink yarn, make a magic ring, ch 1.

Rnd 1: 6 sc in ring, pull ring closed tight (6 sts).

Rnd 2: 2 sc in each st around. Place marker for beginning of rnd and move marker up as each rnd is completed (12 sts).

Rnd 3: *sc in next st, 2 sc in next st* 6 times (18 sts).

Rnd 4: *sc in next 2 sts, 2 sc in next st* 6 times (24 sts).

Rnd 5: *sc in next 3 sts, 2 sc in next st* 6 times (30 sts).

Rnd 6: *sc in next 4 sts, 2 sc in next st* 6 times (36 sts).

Rnd 7: *sc in next 5 sts, 2 sc in next st* 6 times (42 sts).

Rnd 8: *sc in next 6 sts, 2 sc in next st* 6 times (48 sts).

Rnd 9: *sc in next 7 sts, 2 sc in next st* 6 times (54 sts).

Rnds 10-20: sc in each st around.

Fasten off.

EAR FLAP (MAKE 2)

Mark position of Ear Flaps (see page 12). Note: A chain 1 at the beginning of a row is for turning your work and does not count as a stitch.

Row 1: With pink yarn, attach yarn in 1st st with sc, sc in next 6 sts. Place marker for beginning of row and move marker up as each row is completed (7 sts).

Row 2: ch 1, turn, skip next st, sc in next 6 sts (6 sts).

Row 3: ch 1, turn, skip next st, sc in next 5 sts (5 sts).

Row 4: ch 1, turn, skip next st, sc in next 4 sts (4 sts).

Row 5: ch 1, turn, skip next st, sc in next 3 sts (3 sts).

Row 6: ch 1, turn, skip next st, sc in next 2 sts (2 sts).

Row 7: ch 1, turn, skip next st, sc in next st (1 st).

Fasten off. Weave in end.

EDGE TRIM

Rnd 1: Using pink yarn, attach yarn at center back of Hat with sc. Sc in each st around perimeter of Hat making 3 sts at tip of each Ear Flap. Fasten off.

TWISTED CORD TIE (MAKE 2)

Cut six 24" strands of pink yarn. Follow instructions on page 13.

SMALL POM POM (MAKE 2)

With pink yarn, follow instructions on page 14.

EAR (MAKE 2)

With pink yarn, make a magic ring, ch 1.

Rnd 1: 6 sc in ring, pull ring closed tight (6 sts).

Rnd 2: *sc in next 2 sts, 2 sc in next st* 2 times. Place marker for beginning of rnd and move marker up as each rnd is completed (8 sts).

Rnd 3: *sc in next 3 sts, 2 sc in next st* 2 times (10 sts).

Pig

Rnd 4: *sc in next 4 sts, 2 sc in next st* 2 times (12 sts).

Rnd 5: *sc in next 5 sts, 2 sc in next st* 2 times (14 sts).

Rnd 6: *sc in next 6 sts, 2 sc in next st* 2 times (16 sts).

Rnd 7: *sc in next 7 sts, 2 sc in next st* 2 times (18 sts).

Rnd 8: *sc in next 8 sts, 2 sc in next st* 2 times (20 sts).

Rnds 9-10: sc in each st around.

Sl st in next st. Fasten off with long tail.

SNOUT

With pink yarn, make a magic ring, ch 1.

Rnd 1: 6 sc in ring, pull ring closed tight (6 sts).

Rnd 2: 2 sc in each st around. Place marker for beginning of rnd and move marker up as each rnd is completed (12 sts).

Rnd 3: *sc in next st, 2 sc in next st* 6 times (18 sts).

Rnd 4: *2 sc in next st, sc in next 2 sts* 6 times (24 sts).

Sl st in next st. Fasten off with long tail.

TAIL

With pink yarn, ch 16 loosely.

Row 1: 3 sc in 2nd ch from hook and in each ch across (45 sts).

Fasten off with long tail.

ASSEMBLY

Flatten Ears and sew to hat slightly cupped. Sew Snout to Hat. Sew 1/4" buttons to Snout for nostrils. Sew 1/2" buttons in place for eyes. Tie Tail to center back of Hat. Weave in ends. ♦

Templates

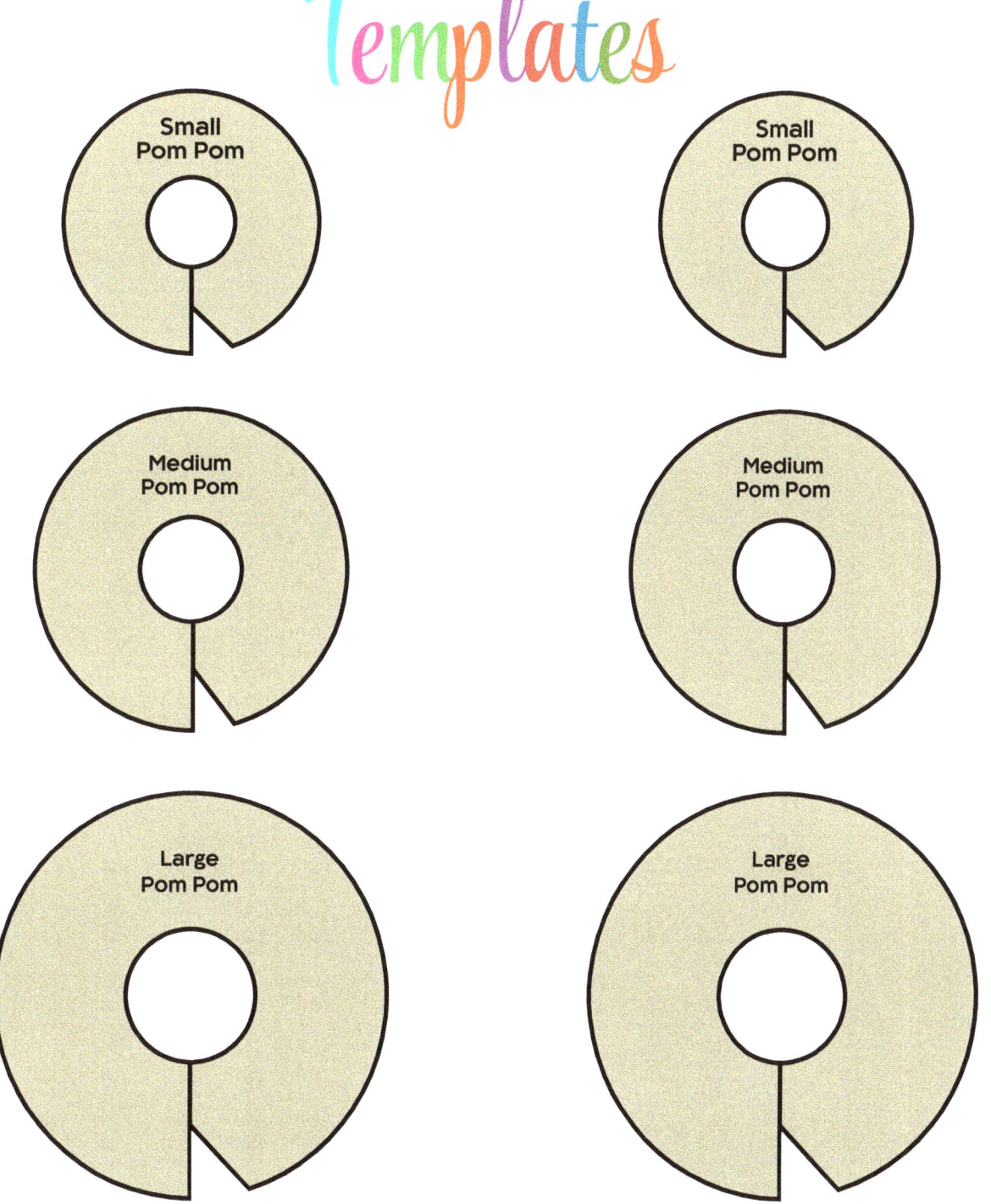

Resources

YARN

Caron Yarn
caron.com
  Simply Soft

Lion Brand
lionbrand.com
  Vanna's Choice
  Cotton Ease
  Martha Stewart Crafts Extra Soft Wool Blend

Red Heart
redheart.com
  Soft

Hobby Lobby
shop.hobbylobby.com
  I Love This Yarn

Michaels
michaels.com
  Loops & Threads *Impeccable*
  Loops & Threads *Soft & Shiny*

Joann Fabric and Craft Stores
joann.com
  Caron *Simply Soft*
  Lion Brand *Vanna's Choice*
  Lion Brand *Cotton Ease*
  Red Heart *Soft*
  Lion Brand *Martha Stewart Crafts Extra Soft Wool Blend*

NOTIONS

Joann Fabric and Craft Stores
joann.com
  Clover *Soft Touch Crochet Hook*
  Disappearing ink marking pen
  Jumbo tapestry needles
  Locking stitch markers
  Knitting counter

BUTTONS

Create for Less
createforless.com

Lots of Buttons
lotsofbuttons.com

VIDEO TUTORIALS

YouTube!
youtube.com
  Search on the name of the stitch or technique you want to learn.

Pinterest
pinterest.com/LindalooEnt/
  Visit my Pinterest page to view video tutorials for the stitches and techniques used in this book. Look for the boards named "Amigurumi Tutorials" and "Embroidery Tutorials".

Featured Yarn

The following yarns were used for these animal hats.

Cat

Lion Brand "Vanna's Choice"
    Color: Silver Gray, #149
    Color: Silver Heather, #405

Caron "Simply Soft"
    Color: Strawberry, #0015
    Color: White, #9701
    Color: Black, #9727

Owl

Caron "Simply Soft"
    Color: Lavender Blue, #9756
    Color: Strawberry, #0015
    Color: Sunshine, #9755
    Color: White, #9701

Sheep

Lion Brand "Martha Stewart Crafts Extra Soft Wool Blend"
    Color: Bakery Box White, #5400

Caron "Simply Soft"
    Color: Black, #9727

Ladybug

Caron "Simply Soft"
    Color: Harvest Red, #9763
    Color: Black, #9727

Lion

Lion Brand "Vanna's Choice"
    Color: Mustard, #158

Lion Brand "Homespun Thick & Quick"
    Color: Natural Stripes, #206

Caron "Simply Soft"
    Color: Black, #9727

Panda

Caron "Simply Soft"
    Color: Coconut, #9601
    Color: Black, #9727

Tiger

Caron "Simply Soft"
    Color: Pumpkin, #9765
    Color: Black, #9727
    Color: Coconut, #9601

Dog

Lion Brand "Vanna's Choice"
    Color: Oatmeal, #400
    Color: Barley, #403

Caron "Simply Soft"
    Color: Black, #9727

Bear

Caron "Simply Soft"
    Color: Taupe, #9783
    Color: Bone, #9703
    Color: Black, #9727

Cow

Caron "Simply Soft"
    Color: Coconut, #9601
    Color: Black, #9727
    Color: Nutmeg, #0013
    Color: Strawberry, #0015

Featured Yarn

Bee

Caron "Simply Soft"
- Color: Sunshine, #9755
- Color: Black, #9727
- Color: White, #9701
- Color: Neon Orange, #9774

Sock Monkey

Caron "Simply Soft"
- Color: Grey Heather, #9742
- Color: Off White, #9702
- Color: Autumn Red, #9730
- Color: Black, #9727

Penguin

Caron "Simply Soft"
- Color: Black, #9727
- Color: Coconut, #9601

Red Heart "Soft"
- Color: Tangerine, #4422

Bunny

Caron "Simply Soft"
- Color: Bone, #9703
- Color: Strawberry, #0015
- Color: White, #9701

Frog

Lion Brand "Vanna's Choice"
- Color: Fern, #0171

Caron "Simply Soft"
- Color: Coconut, #9601
- Color: Strawberry, #0015

Red Heart "Soft"
- Color: Berry, #9779

Chicken

Caron "Simply Soft"
- Color: Coconut, #9601
- Color: Harvest Red, #9763
- Color: Gold, #9782

Octopus

Red Heart "Soft"
- Color: Deep Sea, #9870

Caron "Simply Soft"
- Color: Coconut, #9601

Snow Leopard

Lion Brand "Vanna's Choice"
- Color: Linen, #099

Caron "Simply Soft"
- Color: Black, #9727
- Color: Coconut, #9601

Hobby Lobby "I Love This Yarn"
- Color: Peach, #458760

Dinosaur

Caron "Simply Soft"
- Color: Blue Mint, #9608
- Color: Chartreuse, #9771
- Color: Gold, #9782
- Color: Black, #9727

Pig

Caron "Simply Soft"
- Color: Strawberry, #0015

Other books by Linda Wright

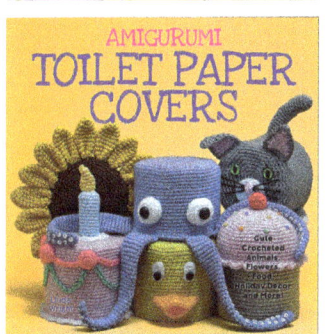

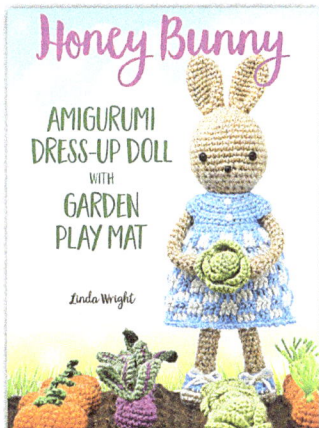

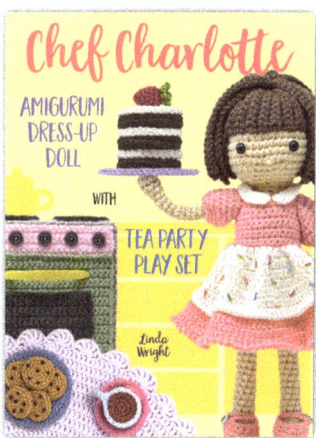

LINDA WRIGHT studied textiles and clothing design at the Pennsylvania State University. She is the author of various handicraft books including the groundbreaking *Toilet Paper Origami*, its companion book, *Toilet Paper Origami On a Roll* and numerous works of amigurumi-style crochet.

Notes

www.ingramcontent.com/pod-product-compliance
Lightning Source LLC
Chambersburg PA
CBHW060935170426
43194CB00026B/2969